To my brother Brian: who made this book possible,
in both the literal and figurative sense.

I pray that all his prayers were answered.

[Edition 2]

VIETNAM UNPLUGGED:

Pictures Stolen – Memories Recovered

Reflections on War While Serving with the 101st Airborne Division

PIERRE (PETE) MAJOR

ISBN: 978-1-09832-089-8 (print)
ISBN: 978-1-09832-090-4 (ebook)

CONTENTS

Forward

This book is the second version which contains 7 new chapters plus additional pictures.

Having said that, more content could have been added, additional stories told, knowing at the same time that the gist of what I wanted said is in the book you hold.

It'll be nice to pull back and get my head out of some of those darker corners of my mind and move on to other projects.

Then there are times when I sometimes think I might return to Vietnam as a tourist, something I've never done since my departure in 1968.

As beautiful as parts of the country are, I'm not sure I'm up to handling the emotional baggage of such a trip.

Still, I never like to say never, we'll see.

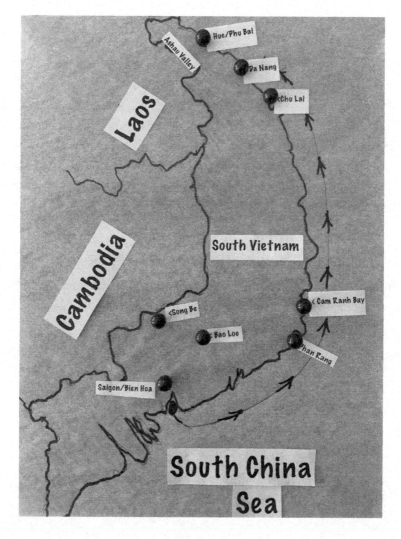

Above

Map of Vietnam and all the locations I operated in during my tour.

The arrows indicate the LST boat that transported us from Saigon to Da Nang after the Tet Offensive.

CHAPTER 1:

The Bank

NINETEEN YEARS OLD AND THE BREAKS WERE FINALLY coming my way.

I would drive my new 400-cube 1965 Buick Wildcat up the circular ramp to the top deck of the Cobo Hall parking lot in downtown Detroit, Michigan. Cobo Hall, which was once the home of the Detroit Red Wings Hockey team and host to the North American International Auto Show and the rock bands Kiss, the Rolling Stones, Pink Floyd, Bob Seger, the Doors, and many more.

The Wildcat was a decent set of wheels, infinitely better than the numerous buses I had been taking to work the past year. Once parked, I'd walk the few blocks over to West Fort Street and Third to start my night shift at one of the largest banks in Detroit. If I was early, I'd detour to have a Coney Island hot dog from a stand a block away, for which Detroit is famous.

While working as a teamster for U.S. Royal Tires on the east side of Detroit, I had been attending night school at the IBM Institute of Detroit. U.S. Royal was a lot of heavy labor in a monster-sized warehouse spanning a block. Its five stories contained tires of every description, everything from Tiger Paw auto tires with the white walls to large aircraft tires.

Prior to completing the course at the IBM Institute, I had been telling everyone there that I would be quitting as soon as my courses were complete. This I did, but without having secured employment first. My Teamster wage of $2.69/hour was big bucks then, and one could raise a family on it. I pounded the streets of Detroit, wondering if I had made the right choice. Thankfully Manufacturers National Bank of Detroit came through. (It has since been bought out by Comerica Bank.)

By contrast, the bank building was a different scene. Not your normal bank building, it housed the bank's data processing center. I was part of a team that worked with an IBM 360 mainframe computer. The 360s were cutting-edge technology at a time when computers were just making their appearance in the commercial world. This was well before PCs, let alone mobile devices.

The 360 took up tons of space and required special air conditioning. Primary storage was kept on large tape drives and magnetic drums, and secondary storage on IBM cards, the ubiquitous punch cards that were all over at the time.

Vietnam, the draft, and everyone's draft status were big concerns in those days. With a double draft deferment, I was able to assure my employers that they need not worry that I'd be taken from them. I was on the ground floor of a career job and life was looking good. Gone were the work clothes that reeked of rubber and on went the suit and tie.

The IBM 360s were unique beasts. One couldn't just go to Best Buy and pick one up. IBM only leased them to large companies for what amounted to thousands of dollars a month plus the expensive service contracts that came with them. No one but IBM CEs (customer engineers) were permitted to "crack the hood" and tinker with the interior. Hard to believe, but even basic handheld calculators had not been invented.

Today I mess around with computers as a hobby, and a micro-controller sitting on my desk which now costs less than $30 could run circles around those 360s. Desktop PCs weren't even on the scene and wouldn't be for another 20 years or so.

Nowadays, stunning advances make their appearance almost weekly. Robotics, drones, graphics, space exploration—it boggles the mind!

Instead of the vast array of programming languages we have to choose from now, then it was mostly just COBOL and Fortran, and maybe assembly language or machine language if you were a customer engineer. Should you go into a bookstore or library in those days, you would be hard-pressed to find a half dozen books on computers. Ask for something about software and you'd get blank stares.

Instead, most of what I learned was in-house training given by the IBM customer engineers on COBOL (a programming language geared to the business community). All very primitive, definitely not user friendly, slow going, and very high on the geek scale. With about four of us in our department working the night shift, we would process the previous day's transactions for loans and discounts. They were to provide the vice president with daily updated reports the coming morning.

We ran literally thousands of IBM cards through sorters, collators, and accounting machines, praying all the while for card jams not to occur. The machines operated at about 600 cards per minute. It was a rare night when a jam on some level didn't happen. Notice of a jam would be announced by the racket of the cards piling into one another in a jumbled mess. Torn, ripped, and mutilated cards would have to be carefully picked out and taken to the Keypunch machine to be reconstructed. Then, with fingers crossed, we'd reinsert them into the stacked piles and resume the operations. Once this whole series of choreographed steps was completed, we marched the cards to a specific individual who used them as input for the 360. There was only one—yes, only one—keyboard for the massive 360. Once processed, the results were printed on large reams of paper tabulating the transactions.

It was critical that the results balance to the penny. If not, it was back to the drawing board to work out the error.

On a good night we could finish in about five hours and then slack off for the remaining three hours of our shift in the employee lounge. A bad night had us stay until the accounts balanced, because we couldn't pawn off our problems on the day shift. We had the occasional long shift.

And now, I went from a cushy job at a bank to being in the infantry with the 101st Airborne Division in Vietnam, during a time when casualties were heavy and in the news daily. How did that happen?

The pay at the bank was good, chances for promotion were excellent, and I could've retired relatively early. What's not to like?

Yes, the work was good—but repetitive and a little boring for my liking. How could I speed up the process?

As it stood, I had been accepted to Wayne State University in Detroit for Electrical Engineering, and the cost of tuition was a factor. Not to mention I was more than intimidated by all the math required when the calculators at that time were slide rules. (Slide rules were modified rulers, a portion of which could be slid to make reasonable mathematical calculations and provide fairly good estimates.)

When I heard Uncle Sam was offering four years of paid college on the GI Bill in exchange for three years of service, well, you better believe I was interested.

CHAPTER 2:

Geographical Overview

———————◆◆—————

UNLIKE MOST OF MANY ARMY AND MARINE DIVISIONS which were restricted to certain areas of Vietnam, our outfit, Company C 2/502, First Brigade, of the 101st Airborne Division, ranged all over South Vietnam. This was to change after I left and my outfit spent much of their time in the A-Shau Valley

As a result, I participated in Search and Destroy Operations covering Saigon to the south, to as far north as Hue and Phu Bai, west along the Cambodian border, and east to the South China Sea. We would be choppered to our area of operation, and from then on everything took place at a blistering slog of about 2.5 mph, if that.

Operating in different parts of Vietnam appealed to the explorer in me. That variety and anticipation of the new took a bit of the edge off the fear of what we might encounter. Travel maps found in travel agencies were replaced by military maps covered with contour lines depicting wild and crazy elevations that could run to thousands of feet. Horizontal and vertical grid lines marked off divisions in square kilometers, or "clicks," as in saying we humped a couple of clicks.

Lessen the weight and remove the aspect of having to be shot at, throw in a few creature comforts, and I would often say "humping" over what in large part is a wild and beautiful country would've been a good gig!

The general term we all used for making our way through the field, jungle, and rice paddies was "humping the boonies." For us, the majority of this was in the Central Highlands, a mountain chain that ran up the spine of South Vietnam. Of varying height and steepness, these mountains and their thick vegetation and cover were brutal to penetrate. Forget roads; a narrow path was a luxury. There was little if any habitation for the most part, save for the indigenous Montagnard tribesmen.

Level ground was rare, and making it up those steep inclines with 60-pound rucksacks was yet another form of ongoing hell. Descending downhill wasn't much relief either. The struggle of ascent was now replaced with what amounted to continual reps of leg squats.

The general foliage was what we referred to as "triple-layered canopy" jungle.

Colors came in green, green, and more green. Colorful flowers were nowhere to be seen, as a rule. Very tall trees, followed by midsize trees, and then the heavy bushes/brush thorns, vines, and elephant grass made up that triple-layered mix. Slipping backwards while climbing, and the reactive motion to latch onto a clump of elephant grass for stability, would often leave you with "paper cuts" as it slid from your sweaty palm.

Very little light penetrated that triple-layer canopy. Throw in low cloud cover and monsoon rains, and it all made for a depressing mix.

We always traveled in single file, the Point Man, or lead, often with his '16 in one hand and a machete in the other, breaking a trail, as the Slack Man covered his flanks. The rest of us followed, trampling out a trail.

Sometimes the height of the mountains was so great that the vegetation and foliage would change before our eyes in the ascent. This was because of the height and cooler temperatures.

A region called Bao Loc fit the bill in this case, and another was by Da Nang. One day that found us ascending forever put us among very tall coniferous pine trees. Not the type of vegetation one connects with Vietnam, but more like you would expect in the Western United States. At this level the weather was noticeably cooler, made more so by the wind. One of our Troopers developed a high fever and we dug a small depression in the ground as protection from the wind until the "dustoff" chopper arrived to take him to the rear. No, it wasn't all heat and tropical temperatures at these heights.

Bao Loc also had some of the steepest, most jagged areas we came across. Crazy vegetation and bizarre terrain were everywhere. I recall going up a steep slope made up of tall trees with the ground carpeted in rocks of all sizes. Strange, and super dangerous. At different stages someone would dislodge a rock and they'd come rolling, bouncing down at you at a speed that could take your head off. How we made it up to the top without anyone injured was a minor miracle.

An area made up of a spongy "floating" carpet of grass covering an area of quicksand was another weird topographical feature. Your foot would sink in and, if you were not quick enough, help would be needed to pull you out.

At times in valleys we would avoid dense underbrush by following small streams, hunched over as we made our way through an overarching tunnel of interweaving vines and branches. The upside of making good time was offset by the downside of the larger water leeches that liked those same streams.

Also in some valleys were rice paddies. Most people are familiar with them. Flooded fields covered with rice plants, divided into plots of random size, and surrounded by berms and dikes to contain and regulate the water levels. One had to be careful not to step on the "cow pies" left by the water buffalo that share those fields.

Exposed and clear of trees, these rice paddies made for ideal ambush zones if you were unlucky to be caught in the open. We avoided crossing them at all costs and usually took the long way around. We didn't venture there too often; that's one positive of operating in the Highlands: not flat enough for rice paddies

Now in another part of the country, just outside Da Nang, I recall a particular mountain. It kept going up, never ending—it could have been Mount Everest, or so it seemed. Constant rain and mist added to our misery. Often what appeared to be the top of the mountain was a "false summit." We'd crest a ridge, have it flatten out somewhat, and then up again we went.

Such was our height that sounds of choppers flying off in the distance started to come from below us, not above as expected. Our radio operators began picking up signals and communications way beyond their normal range.

It was our third day of climbing. By now our platoon had reached the summit. We were in a large expanse of huge trees and undergrowth. The air was in perfect stillness without a wisp of wind—but not just for that moment, it gave off the vibe of never having experienced a gust of wind. Everything that grew was blanketed in dense moss and lichen, some hanging down in long, eerie fingers. The complete and utter silence was broken only by the steady dripping of heavy moisture off trees and long tentacles of moss. Spooky to the max. No North Vietnamese Army (NVA) here, just a setting for Jurassic park, and T-Rex would fit right in. It was definitely right out of another world. There were just two of us that kept going to this point, leaving our squad to rest as we extended our patrol a bit further to see what lay ahead.

It creeped us out, and we decided to rejoin our squad and then our platoon.

Other operations found us among rubber plantations cultivated during French Colonial times. These we saw near the Cambodian border. In flatter terrain and nicely spaced apart, with better visibility than we were used to, it felt more like the forests back in the States in which we played war games. I was hoping to indulge in more of this "level," less stressful type of "humping," when the Tet Offensive cut short our stay in that region and we were brought to Saigon.

The Coastline

Running along the South China Sea, the Vietnamese coastline has many white sandy beaches.

I'd often pick out particular areas that would make beautiful resort areas. Especially near Da Nang and looking down from the mountains to the sea.

Should I ever find myself back in that country, it would be to travel along that coast. The Central Highlands still give me chills at times while reflecting on them. Too many bad vibes there.

CHAPTER 3:

Jump School

———————◆◀—————————

WITH MY LEAVE FROM ADVANCED INFANTRY SCHOOL AT
Fort Dix, New Jersey over, I reported to Fort Benning, Georgia to begin
three weeks of Jump School. When completed, this would give me the des-
ignation of Paratrooper.

Jump school is focused on intense physical training during the first
two weeks, with the final weeks being mostly jumping.

I was looking forward to this. In high school I had been a fair distance runner and could knock off miles all day long. Bring it on!

My first exposure to the whole Airborne (Paratrooper) thing was
in basic training at Fort Campbell, Kentucky. It was home to the 101st
Airborne Division, an elite division with a celebrated history—in particular in the Battle of the Bulge during World War II. Many books and movies
have been made of their exploits of those times.

We would watch from a distance, viewing the jumps as the planes
deployed strings of parachutes billowing as they exited the C-130 aircraft.

A neat feature of Jump School was the fact that it was attended by
military from other branches of the service, not just the Army. Recon
Marines, Navy Seals, even soldiers from other countries were included.
Being all tossed in together allowed us to compares notes as to how these
other branches of the service operated.

First Week

The first week was mostly intense physical training and constantly having to knock out push-ups (20-50) at a time for the slightest infractions.

Drill Instructors (DIs) had to be addressed as Sarge. Lots, of "Yes, Sarge!" and "No, Sarge!" to their requests.

In the Marines, they addressed their Sergeants as "Sir." In the Army, "Sir" was used for Officers.

One Recon Marine in our group was always responding to the DI with "Recon Sir" and not the required "Airborne." This aggravated the DIs and he paid with many push-ups. Gravity always won out.

While on the subject of DIs, midway through my tour in Vietnam our first Platoon Sergeant completed his tour, returning Stateside. To my surprise, who should appear as his replacement—none other than Sergeant H., one of my Jump School DIs. Though he outranked me, by then I was the veteran with more combat experience.

I recall a firefight we were in that had been going on for way too long, ammo running low, the outcome still undecided. Gunships were on their way—hurry up!

The firefight had started at first light and it was now around noon. Sergeant H. made the comment to me that he was losing patience with these NVA because they were cutting into his lunchtime. It was the perfect time for a bit of humor, as the intense stress of the battle was eased by those few words. He turned out to be a decent Platoon Sergeant, and could get the job done, the key requirement in that business.

Back to Jump School. That initial week was like a combination of "tough mudder obstacle race, crossfit gyms, and triathlons"—it was inevitable that some wouldn't make the cut. Those who didn't make the cut (it could be for any number of reasons) were made to do menial jobs around the Jump School while awaiting reassignment orders. Adding insult to injury and to make their status more visible, they were made to wear a yellow helmet while with us.

Yep, the yellow helmet of shame, signifying cowardice. I'm not sure if things have changed these days, but being politically correct wasn't high on Uncle Sam's agenda at the time.

Second Week

This week covered the fundamentals of jumping out of airplanes: aircraft exits and how to land.

Attempting to land standing up was prohibited. We were not skydivers jumping with performance canopies, for whom landing in a standing manner is the norm.

No, keep those knees bent and let the body absorb the impact by rolling to the side and onto your back. Known as a parachute landing fall (PLF). Two separate parachutes were carried. The main chute (T-10) on the back and the smaller reserve in the front around belt level should it be (gulp!) needed.

After some practice of exits at a ground level platform we advanced to the 34-foot tower to perfect our exits there. Picture a water tower with a door and a long zip line and you've got the idea.

Correct exits were needed to insure proper deployment of our parachutes. We would don a harness, and with the zip line secured to our back to simulate a parachute, off we would go. Lots of fun—it's not too often I would use that word in the Army.

The 250-foot tower was the next training aid. It looked like a tower taken from an amusement park. It would hoist you in an already opened parachute to the top. Once released, we would descend to the nice sandy drop zone below. This provides a real life experience with the feel of an actual landing. What it leaves out, however, is the factor that wind can play, spacing between jumpers, and other considerations.

With week two out of the way, it's time to do the real thing: Let's go to week three.

Third Week

The third and final week of Jump School. Five jumps away from graduating.

The first aircraft I jumped from was the C-119, known as the Flying Boxcar. Short and boxy-looking with a double tail, it made for an ideal jump plane. The C-119 was past its prime even then; few remain today.

The fact that it had plenty of clearance by the doors, making a clean exit easier, was a big plus. Nobody wants to have their 'chute snag on the tail. The C-119 carried fewer jumpers, insuring that most would land on the drop zone, not in the trees. Check that concern off the list.

An aircraft held two "sticks" of jumpers, sticks being the row of jumpers exiting the door. One on each side of the plane. After a period of time in which we would be manifested, put on our parachutes, and the safety checks completed, we boarded the plane. Seated and facing each other, we climbed to altitude.

Located by the exit doors were the Jumpmasters. With many jumps and experience they were in command, and would orchestrate the jump once the time came.

That time is now.

"Get ready!" shouts the Jumpmaster. Made more alert, we face each other, awaiting the next commands. The basic web seating and uninsulated surroundings make for a noisy place and it's about to get noisier. Colored lights by the door indicate we have reached jump altitude (approximately 1250 feet). The exit doors on each side at the rear are now opened. If it was loud before, it's deafening now. The thin metal between us and the elements has been removed and the third dimension to the drop zone below is made more real.

"Stand up!" shouts the Jumpmaster, almost inaudible with the engines and rushing wind.

In unison we rise and face the rear of the aircraft.

"Hook up," comes the next command.

We take the snap hook that is attached to one end of our static lines, with the other end draped over our shoulder and coiled on the main chute. We secure the snap hook to a long wire strung the length of each side of the plane.

"Check equipment!"

The final checks are to make sure everything is where it should be and secure, both for yourself and the jumper in front of you.

The Jumpmaster is leaning out, going through his final checks. Leaning out, he scans the aircraft and ground below. Wind speed, aircraft spacing, and approach to the Drop Zone, all have to click. His clothing and the skin on his face is distorted by the exposure to the rushing wind skirting the door.

The next to final command is screamed out: "Stand in the Door!"

The lead jumper in each "stick" takes position in the door, knees slightly bent, a hand on each side of the door.

"Go!" The final command.

Into the prop blast leaps the first jumper, and immediately is hurled back by the wind from the engine. Legs are together and elbows tucked to the side with the hands on the reserve chute.

Like a big centipede, the rest of the jumpers follow in an anxious shuffle and stream out. No turning back now.

The 15-foot static line unfurls and yanks the main chute open. It is four seconds max until the main chute is deployed.

One thousand....

Two thousand...

Three thousand...

Four thousand...

Should you not feel the tug of the deploying canopy, that's the cue to pull the reserve handle on the reserve chute. Exiting at approximately 1250 feet doesn't leave much distance between you and the ground.

Not to worry, the canopy snaps in the air and billows open. It gives a huge sense of relief and elation to have made it through that critical stage.

The noise of the engines, buffeting of the wind, vibration from the C-119, shouting of the Jumpmaster: All that is now replaced by a peaceful silence with the aircraft receding in the distance.

Voices of various soon-to-be Paratroopers carry far in the still air, making comments, and celebrating their survival.

What seemed far away is now taking on a sense of motion with the ground looming larger. Knees bent, eyes focused on the horizon as taught, I brace for impact. In this type of chute, that impact will be made at 17-21 mph—more than fast enough to get hurt.

Thud, toss, roll, tumble, and I made it, still in one piece!

Gathering up my canopy, I make my way to the staging area. Large kits bags are provided to stuff our chutes into. These in turn will be taken back to base and repacked by soldiers whose main job is to do just that.

These Troopers are known as Riggers. Not just our chutes, but those for vehicles and a wide variety of other drops are handled by them.

Hey, that was fun! Finally, an activity in the Army I enjoy!

The Army has a world-class skydiving team known as the Golden Knights. Their sole job is to train for demonstrations and events around the world. Sounds like a good gig. I wonder if they take Troopers who wear glasses? Hmmmm.

Less than a week now and with four jumps remaining to graduation, the end is in sight. The intense Physical Training and harassment of the previous couple weeks has eased off. Most of the remaining days involve chuting up, getting manifested, and assembling by the tarmac. And waiting to board the plane. Pretty much a day-long procedure when dealing with hundreds of jumpers and multiple planes. Now, with an idea of what to expect, making it through my final four jumps and making it to graduation is my sole goal.

That I did, except for the third jump, which could have done me in.

The Third Jump

Yes, the third jump proved to be a challenge.

Once more is was from a C-119. My exit and canopy deployment went fine. I was descending surrounded by countless other Paratroopers all drifting around me at various levels.

The spacing between each jumper varied depending on how we handled the risers. These are straps connecting the harness to the multiple shroud lines leading up to the canopy. The T-10 was the parachute used at the time, and control was very limited. Pull and hold the left riser turns left; repeat for a right turn. It wasn't a radical shift, either, unlike with the sport canopies used by skydivers.

Skydiving is something I tried my hand at many years later. Skydiving ram jet canopies are extremely responsive. Pulling down on those toggle handles was like stomping your foot on the accelerator. A Model T up against a Ferrari.

A little below me and off to my side I see another jumper and the distance between us is closing.

This seems the ideal time to implement a plan that I thought would be cool. I can't remember who exactly planted this concept in my head, but it was obviously someone who knew less than me.

It went something like this. I had heard that if crossing over the top of another canopy, you could more or less "skip walk" across this other canopy with no problem. The idea being that the air contained by the canopy maintained enough pressure to support you.

Yep! I want to hop, skip over the ever-nearing canopy and continue on my way.

Well folks, it's the total opposite. Just at the point I overlapped his canopy from above, the partial vacuum above his chute steals my air, causing my canopy to crumple and momentarily collapse.

Suddenly I find myself enveloped by his chute and I'm all arms and legs flailing away attempting to get out.

With my chute having collapsed, I suddenly drop like a rock. Just in time—with almost zero distance between me and the ground—my canopy reinflates, leaving me barely time to gather my wits and make a shaky landing.

INCIDENT REPORT (taken from *Parachutist Magazine,* published by the United States Parachute Association, which I continue to receive from the time I was skydiving many years later as a civilian). After listing such things as age, sex, time in sport, total number of jumps, and skydives within the last 12 months, then...

Cause of death: Hard landing under a collapsed canopy following a 150-foot drop to the ground. Taken to the hospital with head trauma, fractures, and internal injuries. Died one week later from her injuries.

Articles like this are in the "Safety and Training" section of the magazine near the back. It is done for educational value and is some reading I could have used prior to my third jump. It could've been me that day, or in a wheelchair for the rest of my life.

In no way would I allow myself to even get close to any jumper with my remaining two jumps.

Completing Jump School, the highlight of graduation was the ceremony in which Jump Wings are pinned on our uniforms, designating us as Paratroopers.

Pretty cool.

All these years later, those Jump Wings are one of the few items remaining with me from my time in the Army.

As a civilian, those Jump Wings lived out their life on my keychain.

One day I decided to give them new life and incorporate them into a silver chain bracelet. Off to the jeweler. I now wear it daily.

CHAPTER 4:

Tan Son Nhut

———◆———

LET ME BEGIN AT THE END OF MY TOUR IN VIETNAM.

I'm in the airport waiting lounge at Tan Son Nhut, Saigon (now renamed Ho Chi Min City) waiting for my flight to be announced. My new orders call for me to be reassigned to a yet-unnamed outfit in Okinawa. My Class A uniform lost at the cleaners last minute, I am still dressed in jungle fatigues.

A good portion of the people are military with a nice sprinkling of civilians. I am totally relaxed, not having to walk on the edge of death anymore. Soaking up the good vibes of my surroundings, in a bittersweet way I am ready to put this chapter of my life behind me. Happy and extremely lucky to be leaving with all the body parts I arrived with, unlike many others, a cloud hovers knowing my friends remain in the darkness of the Boonies with more to follow in the months ahead.

The sound of explosions came our way, not too far from the airport, and many people nearby scramble for cover. I remain at ease.

My hearing, one of my more finely tuned senses, instantly recognizes the explosions as "outgoing" artillery fire, as opposed to "incoming," the kind designed to really make you jump.

Those who have scrambled away now drift back to their seats.

Customs and security at departure wasn't as strict in those days, especially within the military. Still, there is a nod to making an effort and we are asked to dump any contraband (dope, weapons of any sort, you name it), no questions asked, into a nearby bin. If you are caught with something past that point, it is off to the stockade. I have nothing to volunteer. Looking back, it would have been nice to bring one of the many possible war souvenirs that passed my way. An AK-47 hanging on my wall would have done the trick.

That small formality taken care of, it came time to board our "7-O-quick," a civilian chartered Boeing 707. In no time, I am in transit to Okinawa, complete with real stewardesses in attendance, and best of all, air conditioning! I am in heaven.

Roughly 1700 miles later, I disembark at Kadena Air Base on Okinawa. In a short time, I find myself before the Army equivalent of the Human Resources Department.

An officer in charge looks over my records and presents me with a choice of postings.

I'm more than a little taken aback by what he offers and pleasantly surprised with this turn of events. Before leaving for Vietnam I had been denied joining the Special Forces and other better positions as I had been told that I couldn't get a security clearance because I was Canadian. Now I am offered that and more. My choices are:

Option A: Special Forces aka the Green Berets. Well...nope. That would have me going right back to 'Nam on any number of "cloak and dagger" missions.

Option B: Noticing on my records that I could type, the officer mentions they need an IBM keypuncher, and asks me if I am interested. Interested! Are you kidding? Visions of a cushy desk job, working in Class A uniform, minimal BS formations or spit and polish.

"But wait, this job requires an even bigger security clearance," I reply.

"Not to worry, we need your skills."

The big rubber stamp comes out and just like that I'm off to my new digs with my newly assigned MOS (military occupation specialty). An MOS is fancy way of saying "job description." Each MOS has a matching combination of letters and numbers, such as Airborne Infantry 11B1P, complete with Top Secret Security clearance.

In no time, I began my new administrative job, leaving the airborne life behind, knocking out IBM cards like nobody's business. (An IBM keypunch machine feeds in a stack of 40 by 80 column IBM cards and punches holes in them using a modified keyboard.)

The work is easy going, the hours great, and promotion comes fast. The bulk of my work consists of transposing daily morning reports onto IBM cards*. In many ways it is a much easier version of my work at the bank prior to enlisting. My boss is a WAC (which stands for Women's Army Corp; women were segregated into their own units at the time). We get along well. I mostly work alone, and if I finish the job early, I am off early. Then it was back to the barracks to change into my "civvies," head off base to the 'Ville and party 'til the Sun rose. Then up around noon to repeat the cycle.

I was off to a nice start in a part of the world that would produce its own set of complications. The complications were different, yet in many ways more challenging, than what I left in Vietnam. Yes, they had just handed me the keys to the candy store, and me, I had a sweet tooth!

CHAPTER 5:

Extraction

———◆———

RELAX, WE'RE NOT GOING TO THE DENTIST.

This is a good type of extraction. It's the term we use to signify the conclusion of a "search and destroy" operation. As a rule, the operation has been in effect for a month or more. All during this time we are out in the Boonies and haven't a clue when the "Brass" will announce its conclusion.

So extraction in this case is the other bookend to the initial part of the start of the operation, which was the combat assault.

It's a date eagerly looked forward to by just about everyone. We're one raggedy bunch by then. Dirty, funky, torn clothing, bug bites, thorn scratches, jungle rot, not to mention the stress of combat taking its toll.

Word finally filters down to our corner of Vietnam that the extraction date is approaching and we'll be heading to a much-needed break in the "rear."

Much of the same preparation that I describe in setting up a landing zone (LZ) for resupply will take place, but in reverse. The big exception is that the "Slicks" will arrive empty to haul us back to the relative safety of the rear area.

A suitable hilltop has been selected as the extraction site. We make our way there and get the machetes out, proceeding to clear it for the oncoming choppers. The hacking and cutting is done with more enthusiasm knowing that we'll be out of here soon. We even make the extra effort to cut all the bush to the proper height to ensure the LZ is approved by the lead chopper.

Our whole company is now assembled and one last task remains. We call it the Mad Minute. It's not howling at the Moon, but better than that.

With our company forming a loose perimeter on the hilltop and facing downhill, we begin discharging our weapons downhill, unleashing a massive amount of firepower. This serves a dual purpose: ridding one of aging (especially the M-60 ammo), tarnished ammo, and discouraging any potential enemy from attempting to sneak up on us.

All this is done on cue. M-16s, M-60s, and M-79s are chewing up the foliage in impressive fashion. This non-firefight is a nice stress reliever as a bonus. With no response from below, we ease off and hold back a bit, saving some ammo should a real firefight develop. Most of us expend half to three-fourths of our ammo. God forbid we really get attacked! Slight chance, but I do have some uneasiness.

Everything is now in place and the Choppers are called and on their way. Yay!!

We see little specks flying in their typical V formation, getting closer and larger.

In standard procedure, a Trooper pops yellow smoke, indicating the LZ for approaching choppers, and positions himself in front with arms up to guide them in.

A chopper swoops in and barely keeps a hover, and a group of four Troopers fight the swirling rotor wash of twigs, grass, and dust and waste no time jumping on. Other choppers rapidly follow, repeating the process.

I'm awaiting my turn when I spot one of my favorite choppers I've seen off and on throughout various resupplies. There is no mistaking it due to its distinctive "nose art." Smack on the nose of the chopper is painted a larger than life size picture of "Little Annie Fannie," a semi-nude depiction of a cartoon female made popular from *Playboy Magazine* at the time.

Similar nose art like this was common in past wars on various fighter aircraft and bombers, and this continued in Vietnam.

I was told later that this particular rendition of Little Annie Fannie was modified somewhat and certain parts of her anatomy were censored by the rear-area "Brass." No doubt a lot has changed in today's military and I don't know if that type of art would be accepted.

My turn to board has come and we scramble on, the Slick follows the hillside down gaining speed, and swoops upward as we gain altitude. A big sense of relief is felt by all. The increased height brings cooler temperatures, making for the best air conditioner I could wish for.

After a period of time the rear area comes into view: heavily fortified military camps with airstrips, rows upon rows of squad tents, and an adjacent town/city. This one is located on the South China Sea, and in better times one could easily imagine a tourist resort situated nearby.

Closer yet, we can see the firebase for the big guns: 155, 175, 8"on tracks. All are capable of reaching many miles into the interior. Piled high and always presenting a tempting target for the enemy are stacks upon stacks of artillery shells in their wooden crates.

We land surrounded by choppers of every sort. Dust is swirling and we pile out crouched out of the reach of the slowing rotor blades. Feels fantastic to be back and everyone is in good spirits.

We expect to be able to grab a breather for about four days and then it'll be off to the Boonies for the next operation. The technical name is known as being on "stand down." We move out to our battalion area to stash our gear in squad tents, themselves not more exotic than something to keep the elements out with a few cots inside and even fewer lights strung overhead.

In the list of priorities, it's "clean your weapons, then clean your ass." So having our weapons cleared and secured, we could now move onto the next item, which for most of us means finding some type of shower and then maybe some beers or other brand of poison.

Our four-day break will pass swiftly and we do our partying while available. We're pretty well exempt from the discipline and spit and polish that is expected of most of the troops stationed in the rear on a full-time basis. Just coming off an operation with another one around the corner leaves nobody in the mood to tolerate any petty harassment.

CHAPTER 6:

Night Ambush

———◆◆◆———

I'D SAY SHE WAS MORE GIRL THAN WOMAN. THE MOON had been coming and going between the clouds. The moment I saw her, the moon had made a brief appearance and lit up an area of rice paddies from where she emerged. I recall her face clearly, and it conveyed an expression of concern if not fear. Young, maybe 15 or 16 give or take, it was hard to say. She was quite close and paused wherever it was she was going. She looked right over my body tucked under the cover of a small bush and my presence went undetected. Wearing just a blouse and a wrap-around sari skirt, her hands were by her thighs holding the sari just above the water-filled rice paddy.

She was alone, with no visible weapon.

Had she come down the trail where the main body of our ambush was situated, she would be killed without question or hesitation. The mass of firepower from the "16s" or booby traps would have seen to that.

Maybe she sensed or knew something was up and was making a detour through the rice paddies? I'll never know. Just the same, she had unknowingly stumbled in the "back door" of our night ambush, where I lay less than 50 yards from the opposite-facing main contingent.

Yet here she was in my kill zone and a decision presented itself. Friend or foe? Shoot or hold? Why didn't I shoot? Because she was a girl? Because she didn't have a weapon?

It was a cardinal rule when it came to firing your weapon at night that you'd better have a dead body to show for it. More than the extreme noise of firing one's weapon is the extreme light given off by the muzzle flash. Once committed, this reveals your location, which can give the enemy a target to zero in on. Not to mention that the element of surprise is lost.

No. My key reason was my weapon at the time was the M-79 grenade launcher. The high explosive single-shot round in my chamber is designed not to activate itself until exceeding a certain distance from the muzzle. This safety feature is in place to prevent the person firing it from being killed or injured by one's own weapon should the round hit a tree limb or any object at close range.

The girl was well within that non-activation radius. It was for that reason I paused.

Then she vanished, as quickly as she appeared, as did the light from the moon. Fate had saved her.

Questions remained. Where did she come from? Why was she alone? What was she doing out so late at night?

Morning arrived without event. I discussed what I saw with the rest of the platoon and no one had noticed a thing.

In hindsight, girl or not, had I killed her many would not lose any sleep over it in our outfit. I might even have received a pat on the back. She would have been viewed as a Viet Cong (VC) sympathizer at best.

A few months later I had swapped my M-79 for the M-16. If I'd had that weapon at the time the outcome might have been different. Where would my conscience be today? I don't know, but no doubt in a more unsettled place. There's no pride or glory in killing an unarmed girl, just the hollow statistic of a body count.

Her guardian angel intervened that night.

CHAPTER 7:

Jacuzzi

———◆———

Location: Phan Rang, On Stand Down.

ABOUT TIME, I THINK. OK, IT MIGHT NOT HAVE BEEN A jacuzzi, but having gone without a shower for the better part of a month, even this setup begins to look like one. This will have to do until I go on R&R.

Our shower construction is very rudimentary. A couple of shipping containers serve as the base on which an empty fuel wing tank from a jet is elevated and a shower head of sorts is rigged.

The very basics—no shower curtain decorated with fish or even an enclosure, for that matter.

Water? It's provided by filling empty Jerrycans. These have a capacity of 5 gallons, which is what we're allocated per person, per shower. If you feel that isn't enough water, you are free to refill and return to the back of the line. The trick is to soap up and rinse off before your single can is drained.

Our platoon stands around in various stages of undress waiting their turn.

Amen, finally my turn.

My luxurious shower now complete, I'm in the process of drying off when I hear a distinct CRACK.

My glasses, which had been sitting on what I thought was a safe place, now lay under someone's Jerrycan. These are my one and only pair, and though intact, the right lens now has a double horizontal crack in it. I am basically blind without them and my heart sinks, hoping the lens will stay put.

Though shatterproof glasses are the norm these days, at the time they were just coming on the scene. In fairness, the army had offered me an extra pair of shatterproof glasses when I was stateside, but my procrastination and not being too crazy about their, shall I say, less stylish selection, added to my delay.

I was extremely near sighted. Back then my eyesight without glasses was 20/400, making me virtually blind without glasses. The fear that my lens could fall out at any time was very real. It could jeopardize my life, let alone my fellow Troopers once back in the boonies.

Before Jump School the army doctor told me that my poor vision had me classed as "non-combat arms," meaning I was to be excluded from a combat role. He had offered me a big "out," but I was able to convince him to let me continue on to Jump School and then an Airborne outfit.

The added stress of not being able to obtain a replacement pair immediately was a huge concern for me. I was assured I could get fitted for a new pair while here in the rear. Not to happen, and I soon found myself choppered out to the Boonies on our next operation, cracked lens and all. It remained that way for the rest of my tour in Vietnam.

Many years later my ophthalmologist told me I had slight cataracts and to consider having them removed. I eventually went ahead with his recommendation and was very pleased to see that the implanted lens replacing them had given me near 20/20 vision. Aside from using glasses for reading, I'm doing great, plus the bonus of big dollars saved no longer having to buy prescription sunglasses.

CHAPTER 8:
Jacuzzi, Continued

WHILE SCANNING MY FAVORITE COMPUTER NEWS FEED, one headline grabbed me and my eyeballs came to a screeching halt. Did I read that correctly? I sure did. The headline read: "Estonian Army always travels with their saunas." The article appeared in the *Wall Street Journal*.

This looked like it couldn't be for real, but it was.

This army has its priorities set right and knows how to conduct a war. No makeshift showers for these guys.

Estonia is one of the three tiny Baltic countries tucked away in Northern Europe. It is one of the countries that had been annexed by Russia after World War II and regained its independence nearly 30 years ago. Their cold winters have long made saunas a part of their culture. So much so that they have devised portable pop-up saunas to take with them wherever they go. Even in the Middle East, including Afghanistan and Israel, where temperatures can get quite toasty. The interior of a sauna can exceed 200° F, but the logic is that once you climb out into 110° F, it seems cooler given the heat of the sauna. Makes sense to me.

The whole sauna ritual is an established tradition in Estonia and many of the Nordic countries. It's considered essential for cleansing not just the body but the spirit. Maybe this is a tradition we could adopt. I'm sure the military could have it on their recruiting posters as a selling point.

I'm tempted to pile on loads of puns here, but I'll leave it for the readers to create some.

Meanwhile, back to 'Nam, where we find ourselves in the Boonies. Need to pee? Find a tree, simple enough.

For no. 2, no problem. Get out your entrenching tool (shovel), and with a scoop or two we have an instant "outhouse." Toilet paper is supplied courtesy of our C rations. Refill the hole and you're on your way.

On one occasion I found myself going through the above procedure and sunk my entrenching tool into the soft earth. I lifted up a good chunk of dirt and what do I uncover? Nothing less than a nest of tightly entwined baby snakes all writhing together.

Poisonous or non-poisonous, I don't know, but I'm not waiting around for their mom to show up.

I quickly replaced the dirt on top of them and walked a few yards away to take my business elsewhere.

Another danger lies in being walked up on by the enemy in a compromising position. I've known this to happen to at least one individual. Just so you know that there are more than snakes to be aware of.

At our main base camps in the rear areas, the latrines were slightly more sophisticated, though in reality they amounted to little more than glorified outhouses. They are wooden shacks, extended to accommodate multiple toilets. Rather than a hole in the ground, 55-gallon drums cut to the appropriate size serve as a removable "honey bucket."

When these honey buckets were eventually filled, there is a quick and easy solution. At the rear of these sheds, hinged doors were installed, allowing access to the drums.

Using a long hooked wire, the "buckets" were dragged out a few yards. From there, it was a simple matter of pouring diesel fuel into the drums, lighting a match, and stepping back.

Who knew poop could be so combustible, yet it is. And as a bonus, it doesn't give off the expected offending odor. Before long it's burnt to a crisp, leaving just a few ashes. With the drum flipped over and ashes tapped out, the drums are returned to the shack. Voila!

Having once been selected to do the above detail, I can say it wasn't that bad, and for sure I've had worse.

As a nod to a more creative take on designer urinals, in one rear area location expended 105 howitzer shell casings were used. With them propped up on end, we peed into the open part. At eye level and written on a board were the words "shoot low." A double reminder of sorts. An addition to the current job was to keep the barrels of our '16s low when firing on full automatic. An M16, when fired on full automatic, had a tendency to "ride up" in the heat of combat. Hence, hold it firm and shoot low.

Speaking of urinals, I am almost asleep on the ground one evening in the rear area, with the total darkness of a blackout, when my slumber is interrupted with a slight rain. But wait, skies are clear. That's not rain, what the hell.

Not paying attention, a drunk GI had wandered my way and unawares, decides to relieve himself inches from my head, urine splashing on my face. Yuk!

"Sorry man," is the best he could say as I cursed him out. Puts a different twist on the phrase "rude awakening."

Fortunately the following day we were all in for a treat. Our company had a rare opportunity and we all hopped onto deuce half-trucks and were taken to the beach. I'm talking about the South China Sea here. Saltwater or not, I took a bar of soap with me and used this rare opportunity to give myself a good head-to-toe scrub down. I can't tell you how good this "bath" felt.

For most of us, a real good bath or shower would have to wait until R&R, a two-week vacation inserted somewhere in the course of a tour and eagerly looked forward to by one and all. We took R&R on an individual basis and could pretty well choose from a list of possibilities, such as Singapore, Bangkok, and Sydney, to name a few.

Returning from R&R and coming back to what we knew awaited us in the Boonies was another story.

CHAPTER 9:

Stolen Photos

———◆———

HAVING VERY FEW PHOTOS FROM THIS TIME TO REMI-
nisce over was a prime reason for writing this book. Not that I didn't take
some photos, but they were taken from me by a universal condition that
affects all walks of life: theft. The sting is all the worse when done by those
close to you in an unexpected manner.

Of the half dozen times in life where I've been robbed, it was usually
when I had an awareness of what could happen and took precautions.

Once at a gym playing indoor soccer, a whole bunch of us had our
car windows smashed. Glove compartments were gone through and ran-
sacked. Not leaving my wallet in such an obvious place but in another part
of the car saved me then.

Playing hockey in a different location, we returned to change after
the game and found our lockers broken into. Again my loss was minimal,
if only because I was too broke in those days to be flush with cash. It made
sense to us in hindsight why there was such a noisy, enthusiastic cheering
section of kids at one end of the rink. Turns out they were decoys and spot-
ters for the thieves.

Maybe I'm naturally more aware, but I'm amazed at how many people can take such a casual approach to their belongings from the standpoint of security. Whether it's leaving wallets or purses unattended or
"flashing your roll" with an obvious display of your cash and wealth, you

make yourself a target to thieves who are more than willing to separate you and your riches.

Later as a civilian and working in the trucking industry, I'd always be blown away by the casual approach to security taken by many truckers.

Go to any truck stop and you'll find many trucks idling unattended, keys in the ignition and just asking to be taken down the road by crooks. And they are. Tractor trailers valued in excess of hundreds of thousands of dollars, not to mention freight they carry that could well exceed those figures, make it one of the most lucrative areas of theft.

Fill out a police report and they'll add it to the many already in their files. The police will tell you that chances are slim to none that any of it will be recovered.

In Vietnam, theft visited me twice.

In Phan Rang, we've just returned from the boonies. Rucksack, weapons, and the rest of our gear is stashed in the squad tents. I've removed my bedroll from my rucksack. It contains my poncho, poncho liner, and my undershirt, having placed it on my cot.

Troopers come and go. Locks aren't necessary, with nothing of value to be had. Little money is carried by any of us. A small amount maybe for incidentals, but the bulk of our money we withhold, and it sits accumulating in our accounts.

Returning from wherever, I sit on my cot aware that my bedroll has been disturbed. I immediately notice that my Long John undershirt is missing. Did I say nothing of value was missing? Value is a relative term in this case, and my undershirt was very, very valuable and a prized item of clothing. In terms of monetary value you wouldn't pay $5 for it if you came across it in a yard sale. In fact you'd move away quickly given that it hadn't been washed in at least three months. Still, it was in relatively good condition with no holes or tears. It had been issued to us a while back to ward off the chill we encountered at higher levels in the Central Highlands. Reaching the top of many a high peak in the Boonies, sweat pouring off my body, having that tiny layer of warmth to put on as the cool air settled in would now be missing.

It wasn't stolen by anyone in my platoon; still, it was done by someone who knew its value.

Theft, the second instance;

With my time remaining "in country" down to less than a couple of weeks, I underwent the standard process where I awaited my new orders reassigning me to my new outfit, yet to be determined.

This was taking place in Bien Hoa, the new rear area for the 101st Airborne. I liked our old base camp at Phan Rang situated on the South China Sea. Bien Hoa, Saigon, Long Bing, and Tan Son Nyut Airbase were all part of a sprawling military and civilian complex in the Mekong Delta.

I was days from my departure (DEROS) and I had turned in my M-16, ammo, and related gear.

For the time being I was also detached from the 101st and barracked with troops of unrelated units undergoing the same process. We called it a RepelDepel, short for a Replacement company, like being in a state of limbo during a short period of transition.

No hassles, no work details. Just chill and hang out waiting on the new orders to arrive that came in on an individual basis, at any moment. When they did, I'd be boarding that 707 and out of there.

Our one obligation was to assemble up for morning formations where Roll Call would be taken.

Our gear was stowed in our individual duffel bags and lay on bunks unattended, in an actual building no less.

I returned from one routine roll call and went to my bunk when I picked up on something being out of order. Not just my duffel bag but many others had been opened, clothing spilled out and in my case, more. My used '60 ammo can, a sturdy storage container in which I had kept undeveloped rolls of film all accumulated from my Brownie Instamatic camera, was now gone. Not taking the chance of losing my undeveloped film in the mail, I had stashed these rolls to take home for later processing and developing.

Many pictures taken of me, friends in my outfit, loaded down with rucksacks and weapons. Pictures taken of enemy weapons from recent fire-fights. Pictures of different geographical features, that and more, all gone.

My feelings fluctuated between intense anger against whoever had done this and the sadness of the memories stolen from me. Once again, the dollar value was minimal, but the personal loss couldn't be measured.

CHAPTER 10:

Tet Offensive

———————◆—◄———————

IN TERMS OF SCALE, IT WAS THE AMERICAN FORCES' largest single engagement with the Viet Cong/NVA at the time. The attacks were bold and totally unexpected.

It took place over the course of the lunar (Tet) new year in 1968, beginning at the end of January. Most major towns and cities in South Vietnam were attacked simultaneously. U.S. Military bases throughout the country took a pounding.

Our Company was operating near the Cambodian border at the time, and our newly set up firebase was being hit throughout the day and evening. That night we managed to hold off an assault by point-blank firing of our 105 howitzers into the tree line just beyond our perimeter.

The urgency to redeploy us to the Saigon area the next morning took precedence over us even checking out the battlefield for enemy dead. Something strange was up.

Our orders were to pack up and go, ASAP. We filled in and destroyed our well-built bunkers and defensive positions. Choppers arrived and hooked up the 105s to slings underneath them. Then it was our turn to hop on other choppers.

Tons of activity and little in the way of answers to our questions of what's going on. In truth, no one had answers at that time, such was the scale and confusion of unfolding events.

I vaguely remember us being choppered to a central staging area with a huge number of aircraft of every description coming and going. Then they piled us into C-130 transport aircraft that took us to Saigon, which had been experiencing heavy enemy contact.

While boarding the 130, I tripped and my elbow smacked the concrete, leaving me with a bad bruise. Disembarking from the same aircraft, it was discovered to have a flat tire.

A bad landing for both of us.

At one point the grounds of the American Embassy had been breached and it was Troopers from our sister Battalion, the 327, 101st Airborne, who landed on the embassy roof and worked their way down the stairs to secure it.

The fighting in the Saigon area was very heavy until we gained the upper hand.

By the time we got there, however, most of the city had been retaken and fighting quieted down for the most part. Manpower was spread thin.

To extend our defensive perimeter the first night there, I was paired off with a U.S. soldier from an unknown rear-area unit with zero combat experience. Though he was a nice enough person, I wasn't thrilled having to spend a night in a foxhole with someone untried in combat. At least I was spared the work detail some of us had of collecting dead VC from the surrounding area.

Further attacks that night didn't come about. We spent the evening viewing gunships strafe targets in the distance, in itself a reassuring distraction. Firing at 6,000 rounds per minute, the tracers would descend in red streaks as they raked the ground below, and the buzz-saw sound would then follow. Back and forth the firing continued.

My new buddy for that one evening had some sort of Top Secret MOS, and try as I might, he would not reveal to me what his job entailed. It definitely wasn't Infantry as I had to give him a crash course on basic tactics—not too reassuring from my standpoint.

We spent that night in our foxhole with me trying to get him to crack and tell me what his job was. He didn't give in, and left me wondering to this day what the hell could be that critical.

So other than tripping while piling on board of the C-130s earlier that day and landing painfully on my elbow, Tet was a big non-event for me. I had been in the eye of the hurricane initially, but in the gathering of our overwhelming firepower, their retreat was inevitable.

Bit of a bummer at the time. I was still fairly gung ho then, and having an open field of fire on the enemy was a step up from stumbling into each other in dense jungle.

We spent the next couple of weeks or so making sweeps of the surrounding area, but the enemy was totally defeated, and those not killed retreated back to the Boonies.

Another quirky thing that stood out in my mind was talk of us maybe being issued more presentable (cleaner) uniforms. This was because our usual ragtag scruffy jungle fatigues might have presented a less than desirable view to the American public should we be caught on television by a passing war correspondent.

Our response to that was to hell with those "REMFs," this is combat, not a movie set. F*** you, we don't put up with that BS here. Lucky for them, it didn't come about.

So, as in any battle big or small, ten or ten thousand combatants, an infantry soldier sees only what's in his range of fire. Such was my window on the Tet Offensive. It was only much later that all the facts sorted themselves out and the Tet became known the way we see it now.

Most major towns and cities of any size were attacked simultaneously. Initially caught by surprise, American forces recovered enough to take those places back.

The ancient imperial city of Hue situated up north was another story. The fighting was intense and vicious. It was made more difficult, since the central part of the city contained an old citadel with heavy walls and fortifications. The Marines there faced tough street fighting, taking a lot of casualties; it was a good month before Hue was secured.

We passed through there a month or so later and the place was devastated. I don't think I saw one building or structure without pockmarks, scarred from bullets and explosions.

A large segment of civilians, over 2,500, were said to have been massacred for the short time the NVA held Hue. Thousands more were killed in the fighting. Another example of how civilians can be caught in the middle and how those suspected of working or sympathizing with the United States were shown no mercy.

Sadly the same goes on today. The U.S. will make big promises to interpreters and various staff working to aid us in war zones that we're involved in overseas. We give them assurances of safety and promises of residencies in the United States. When it comes time for us to pull out, they and their families are left hung out to dry at the mercy of the opposing sides as they are locked in a battle of paperwork, visa applications, endless forms to be filled out, and waiting, caught by the changing whims of political parties.

It's Dante's Inferno of bureaucratic hell.

Their pleas to have our promises honored might hit the back pages of newspapers or the radio if they're lucky. Knowing first-hand the consequences they will suffer often leads me to switch the radio station.

New politicians are voted in. Old promises go out the window, petty politics and turf wars replace the real war.

But back to Vietnam.

So, who won the Tet Offensive?

It's generally agreed that from a military standpoint, the United States and its allies did. But the fact that the North Vietnamese and Viet Cong were able to mount such a massive countrywide offensive is contrary to what the American public had been told about the enemy. From the greater political perspective, the North Vietnamese got the upper hand.

Total American service personnel in Vietnam at that time topped 500,000. The top Generals requested more troops, and that didn't fly with the American public. Public opinion was rapidly shifting. Even with my narrow window on the overall picture then, I noticed a trend. The writing was on the wall—our days in Vietnam were numbered.

CHAPTER 11:

Spaghetti Cannon

———————◆———————

I WAS ABOUT TEN AT THE TIME. WE LIVED IN SUMATRA, Indonesia, as my father was working for Standard Mobil Oil at a refinery there. U.S. and Canadian foreigners lived in a compound separated and somewhat insulated from the poverty and lifestyle of the local population.

My brothers and I played with our toy soldiers, small spring-loaded cannons and Dinky Toys army trucks. If you're from England, you know what Dinky Toys are, no explanation required.

One of my father's friends was a chief engineer who worked on a "tramp steamer" that plied the local waters. He would bring us cool toys from Singapore when his ship docked at the refinery. My Meccano set and Lionel train gave me the most fun.

The captain of that same ship would allow the older high-school-age kids to swing from the ship's bridge on a rope to another area of the deck, and it didn't get any cooler than that! The ship wasn't as big as the larger oil tankers docked in the same area but it made for an ideal pirate vessel in our fantasies.

Then as now, the Malacca Strait between Sumatra and Singapore was notorious for actual pirates. It's a narrow shipping lane connecting the South China Sea and Indian Ocean. Anyone who is the captain of a ship had to know what they're doing to work in that setting, be it one of the large container ships seen today let alone a smaller vessel.

Returning from the first two-year stint of my dad's job in Indonesia, we went through that same Malacca Strait on an Italian ocean liner and continued through to the Indian Ocean. We passed through the Gulf of Aden, past Yemen, and into the Red Sea, even more prime pirate zones in those unstable times.

Our ship stopped in Aden as we went on a little tourist excursion. I remember my parents giving me the serious "stick close and don't go wandering off" talk. I was very impressed with the huge surrounding mountains and all the men with wicked, curved daggers in their belts. Yemen is now a hot war zone along with many of its surrounding neighbors.

Luckily we made it without incident, and our only casualty was my stomach as we crossed the Mediterranean Sea to Italy. I got seasick as a dog.

Back to my toy cannon.

I wasn't having much luck with accuracy, just lots of random hits and misses.

Then I got an insight. Why don't I calibrate the distance of the toy cannons? I put the barrel level with the floor and made my shells, spaghetti and macaroni pieces, all the same length. That done, I found that my "shells" all went about a yard.

When my brothers weren't around, I measured the distance of the cannon's muzzle to their soldiers.

The battle started up again and I was knocking down their toy soldiers with 95% accuracy. My brothers were astounded, it was no contest. They couldn't believe I was such a great shot.

Could it have been that artillery was my calling in the military? The whole ballistics end of it held a certain appeal to me. Making a career out of it didn't hold the same attraction.

The Big Guns

The 155s and 175s artillery pieces were too big to just hitch up to the back of your pick-up truck and take off down the road. With their long-range capabilities they didn't need to move.

For the most part they remained in the rear areas, with "Fire Missions" radioed in by Forward Observers in the field. Wooden crates of their shells would be piled nearby that rivaled the pyramids in height. Somewhat protected by sandbags, they remained juicy targets for mortars and rockets.

These would sometimes be set off in mortar and rocket attacks. The resulting explosions could go on for hours. A single high-explosive shell is extremely deadly. Light a match to the hundreds and you could imagine the devastation and chaos.

Eight-Inch Guns on Tracks

I was seated somewhere off to the front of an eight-inch gun on tracks, one of the larger artillery pieces capable of reaching distances of 5 plus miles with ease.

I was about ready to dig into a hot meal prepared by one of our field kitchens and picked a spot on a slight hillside some 300-400 yards off the front of the eight-inch gun. It was making preparations to fire at a distant target well inland.

I thought I might as well enjoy the impending fireworks while chowing down.

Then the crew of the eight-inch gun began yelling in my direction along with lots of animated waving of arms.

I couldn't make out what it was they were trying to communicate, but I had a rare hot meal on my lap that was my priority.

The gun crew fired the round, BOOM!

The immediate shock wave and concussion from the firing let me know in no uncertain terms what all the fuss was about.

I had been within range of the effects of the muzzle blast.

I needed no convincing as to my next move, and move I did as I picked up my tray, ears still ringing, to a less-exposed viewing spot.

Illumination Rounds

I recall a particular time in the Chu Lai area where we were under threat of being attacked with mortars nightly. The vegetation was a little more open, lots of elephant grass, and we could see open area into the valley below.

Well, we couldn't really see anything, but illumination rounds solved that for us. Fired artillery from a distant location, they were designed to do what the name implied, illuminate the area. The rounds would come whistling in, the canister containing and releasing a flare attached to a small parachute. White, red, green—in different colors the flares would make their slow descent to the ground at varying levels, often taking minutes.

It would be enjoyable to watch if it wasn't for the stress of scanning the hillside below for NVA.

Looking to my left or right I could just pick out other foxholes with a fellow Trooper that made up our perimeter.

Other times similar illumination rounds were dropped by circling fixed-winged aircraft high above. The effect was the same, a half dozen or so parachute flares making slow descents at random levels, the light and shadows fading in and out.

The mist formed in the valleys far below. It was spooky in a comforting sort of way, the faint whistling of the flares descending, the soft light and shadows.

I can't remember the type of planes used or the outfit involved. Only their slogan: "We turn night into day and keep it that way."

They certainly did a great job of that.

CHAPTER 12:

82nd Airborne

———————◆————————

THE PATCH FOR THE 82ND AIRBORNE DIVISION, OUR
Division, had "AA" on it for "All American."

This part of my life predated Vietnam and was the first regular unit I
was assigned to after my initial training. I arrived with the rank of Private
First Class (PFC) with an MOS of 11B1P, Airborne Infantry. With an
MOS like that, it was almost a sure bet that one has a reservation on a 707
to Vietnam.

The 82nd Airborne Division is located at Fort Bragg near Fayetteville,
North Carolina, and was one of the two Paratrooper Divisions in the U.S.
army at the time. The other was the 101st Airborne Division located at Fort
Campbell, Kentucky.

The First Brigade of the 101st was already in Vietnam then, and
would be the outfit I was to join later as a replacement, sent there on an
individual levy. In addition to providing many of the replacements to
the 101st in Vietnam, the 82nd also served as the unit for many Vietnam
returnees from the 101st and 173rd Airborne Brigades once their year-long
tour in Vietnam was complete.

My barracks in the 82nd was a big block-like building that housed a
whole company, comprised of four platoons. NCOs, or Non-Commissioned
Officers, lived in semi-private quarters and the rest of us peons in large,
open dorm areas. Officers lived in different quarters entirely.

Double bunks were arranged in two rows with a main aisle running down the middle. Once our bunks were made up in the morning with the blankets stretched skin tight, they couldn't be sat on or laid on until after 6 p.m. No kicking back and snoozing in that unit. Try it and you'll find yourself on KP (kitchen patrol).

Everything was spit and polish in an Airborne unit at that time. Uniforms were cleaned and starched and hours were spent cleaning things seen and unseen many times over, whether it was boots, dishes, floors, latrines, weapons, or uniforms.

Every morning was the same routine. Up at 0500, a half hour of physical training (PT), followed by forming up in platoons, companies, and then most of the division to set out for a two-mile jog doing the "Airborne shuffle." It looked impressive, as most of the division wound their way up and down the streets singing and calling out cadence to keep time. There would be literally thousands of Paratroopers every morning and we looked badass. Cadence would be called out to maintain synchronization, repeating things that would land us all in jail today. My platoon was almost all black except for four or five of us white boys. Yes, I did manage to muster up some rhythm. Had we had YouTube at the time, we could've sent a video of what we looked and sounded like to the NVA in Vietnam and impressed them enough to lay down their arms. I wish war was that easy.

Situated right by Fort Bragg is Pope Air Force Base. I was to see a fair bit of Pope Air Force Base while making my jumps as a Paratrooper; it was where I did most of my jumps. By far the C-130 troop transport plane was the most used for those jumps. A large four-prop plane, it held at least 60 Paratroopers. By jump, I mean you sort of walk out the door at an angle, protected by a jet exhaust deflector. On one occasion I did manage to jump out of a C-141 Starlifter, a large troop and cargo jet. It has since been replaced by a newer jet model.

Contrary to our badass reputation, many Paratroopers were reluctant to jump and did the bare minimum to maintain their jump status to qualify for the extra pay, a whopping $55 per month, which was big money back then.

I took the other approach, and would volunteer to do more jumps. I wanted to become better at it and it was a good change of pace from the routine detail work I might otherwise be doing. I welcomed the opportunity to see if I could jump from different aircraft; everything from choppers to jets (C-141) were on the table.

Being placed on a manifest for a jump and heading down to Pope Air Force Base was a day-long procedure. Drawing our parachutes and reserves, manifesting, heading down to the tarmac, going through the safety checks, and waiting on the aircraft, all took time.

The T-10, the standard military parachute at the time, was very limited as to control of the canopy. It lacked the extra toggle handles that I used many years later in skydiving to steer or stall the canopy.

The parachute landing fall (PLF) we were taught in jump school was enforced. No fancy stuff like trying to land standing up.

Our drop zones, or DZs, around Pope were pretty forgiving. Sandy, they offered a bit of a cushion from the PLF.

Still, given the number of jumpers, various wind conditions, and number of aircraft that could be jumping at one time, sprains, broken bones, and concussions weren't uncommon. Oh, and death was always a possibility.

These thoughts were to be avoided while sitting on the tarmac waiting for aircraft or riding up to jump altitude. Better to light up a cigarette (allowed back then) and try to look nonchalant.

At Pope there was always the constant background noise of planes and jets taking off and landing.

Once on the aircraft, that noise was greatly magnified by the lack of insulation and creature comforts you find on commercial planes. The vibration of the four engines was noticeable throughout. Facing each other, seated on web seats in two "sticks," we could barely hear each other talk.

At jump altitude, the noise turned to a roar once the Jumpmaster opened the door. The roar of those engines made yelling the only communication option. Given the "go" to exit, the "stick" would start moving and there was no stopping it.

The jumping altitude was just over 1,200 feet. It seemed high at the time, but when I consider the 14,000-foot exit altitude I was to later jump while civilian skydiving (I would pull the ripcord at approximately 5,000 feet), it left little room for error.

I managed to add nine or ten jumps to the five from jump school before I got my orders for 'Nam.

Not a great amount when one considers the hundreds to thousands of jumps skydivers commonly rack up. Still, military jumping offers unique twists that can't be obtained anywhere else, plus the fact that's it's on their dime.

My dreams of maybe moving up the food chain and joining the Golden Knights, the Army Skydiving Team, were brought to a close when my orders for 'Nam came down. I'm not sure they would've accepted someone wearing glasses in any event.

The 82nd Airborne Division was my first assignment to a regular outfit once my initial training was complete.

As a point of reference, let me say that when our family first moved to the United States, it was to a suburb of Detroit called West Dearborn (as opposed to East Dearborn, big difference). My father took a position at Marathon Oil and at the time, West Dearborn was a middle to upper middle class all-white suburb. The mayor of West Dearborn had been the longest-running mayor of any town in large part because he was able to maintain its status quo despite being adjacent to Detroit, a majority black city.

Back to the 82nd. I report to my company and discover my newly assigned platoon is majority black (though "Negroes" was the word used at the time). Of the 50 or so in my platoon, there were just five of us white boys (or ace cats, whiteys, honkeys, grays, just a few of the names used for us). Of those five, two became my friends, and another had been reassigned from the National Guard and was a non-Paratrooper. He was bullied incessantly because of it.

The remaining white boy was a card-carrying Nazi who wasn't shy about his views. He'd get comics books with the front cover displaying art that read "Whiteman battles the Jew from outer space." You'd think he would cool it, since we had gang members in our platoon, men from the Blackstone Rangers, Vice Lords, and Black Panthers. No, he once got into a verbal dispute that had him throwing gas on the fire by him saying, "I'm free, white, and 21." That was it; a few black dudes put the "hurt" on him and he kept his opinions to himself from then on. Still, that didn't stop him from occasionally trying to convert me to his thinking. Not for me!

"Cherries" like myself got picked on and bullied initially until the pecking order was established (through fights, of course.) Another category of troops (if you want to call it that) that we had in our company was classed as "Vietnam returnees," combat veterans normally, who had serviced with the 101st or 173rd Airborne. You could tell they were different, usually quieter, kept to themselves for the most part. Nobody messed with them.

One, PG, became my friend. He had served with Charlie Company, the very same one within the O'Deuce I was to be assigned to in a few months. At the time he served there, his Commanding Officer (CO) was Captain Carpenter. Charlie Company was involved in an infamous battle that took place at Dak To. With superior numbers, the NVA had just penetrated the perimeter. In a last-ditch attempt to stop them, Captain Carpenter called jets in to bomb his own position. Big casualties resulted on both sides, but the NVA were halted. That battle made big news Stateside, with armchair generals, civilian and military, weighing in as to whether it was the right call. PG thought it was. It was that or death.

My friend PG was forever trying to impress on me the severity of what I would be up against if I were to go to Vietnam. I didn't have a clue. Until you experience war first-hand, none of us do.

Just the same, it remained a very stressful environment and would get really crazy on weekends. Drinking, drugs, fights, knives, those wicked "straight razors" most of the blacks in our outfit carried, and the trash talk that went with it made me constantly wary. Playing the 'dozens', super loud music played on weekends, GI's playing poker, craps. Yes folks, a far cry from West Dearborn. Other than two or three serious wackos, I got along with everyone else.

Designated as an assistant gunner for the M-60, I was a low man on the totem pole. At times we'd go out to the field and play war games. Some of these could get serious and were a little more war than games. In one instance in Pennsylvania, we had snuck up on and captured a designated opposing unit and one guy had his weapon inches from his stomach. Not coming along quietly, he yelled out a warning and was promptly shot point blank in the stomach with a blank. Blank or no blank, at that short distance it will pierce the skin. We took off running and made our escape.

Being the main Paratrooper Division in the United States, the 82nd always had at least a battalion on call and ready to board aircraft to any hot spot in the world. Within the division, different battalions rotated this responsibility and when doing so, had to stand in full gear and weapons, ready to go at a moment's notice. Which is to say that we had to hang around the company area.

Poker and craps were big in our company. We had dudes who were brought up rolling dice, the way other kids the same age were rolling around their wooden blocks. I would stay away from dice, but not poker—I like a good poker game. With one poker game that went on way too long, I lost what amounted to my paycheck. It wasn't a huge chunk of change; however, paydays were a month apart then and I really had to tighten my belt between paydays from then on.

I was never a gambling addict as some were. For those who were always short of change and needed money to tide them over, another friend of mine had a good side income as a loan shark to those in need. He was a nice guy but come time to collect on his debts, you had best have your money ready. No excuses.

A few months went by and eventually, without surprise, my orders come down.

I was being reassigned to the First Brigade, 101st Airborne Division in Vietnam as a replacement to what ended up being Charlie Company 2/502, with the 3rd Platoon, known by us as "Fletcher's Fighters" after the name of First Platoon Sergeant, Sergeant Fletcher.

With my short leave over, I flew out of Fort Lewis, Washington in cool fall weather on a civilian-chartered Boeing 707. In no time I was walking down the gangplank, disembarking into intense heat at Cam Ran Bay, Vietnam, the prime entry point for most troops at the time.

CHAPTER 13:

ETS

—➤◆◄—

ETS STANDS FOR END TERMINATION OF SERVICE.

After Vietnam, my remaining time in the Army was spent in Okinawa. My initial arrival there felt like Heaven. After a week of just staying on base and savoring long-overdue showers and a real bed, it was time to go to town and check out the Ville.

The Ville might just as well have been a store called "Sex, Drugs, and Rock & Roll," one I entered and didn't walk out of until my ETS months later.

I lived off post, had a "jam" job doing data entry, no spit and polish, getting promotions. Life was good! One big party.

While there I managed to further complicate my life in ways that made Vietnam seem a better option.

The day I thought I'd be looking forward to was now here (ETS), and I felt like I had just been spit out through one of those "time portals" seen in SciFi movies and come tumbling to rest from another dimension.

In this case the portal was Oakland, California. I was a civilian once more.

Gone were all the wild and crazy things I had been involved in. Gone were the people who I was connected to and now replaced with a new set of folks totally unaware of the events taking place on the other side of the world.

A few hours earlier I had been in Okinawa, in the departure area of Kadena Air Force Base standing around the airport waiting for my flight home.

I was gathered around a TV along with a number of other military personnel watching an impending historic trip of a different kind. The first manned trip to the moon was about to launch. As a rule I'd be interested in that type of thing, but not then.

I was bummed out big time. My thoughts were distracted by leaving my pregnant girlfriend and all the emotions that entailed.

ETS. Three big letters that says one's time in the Army is up. It's official, the gig's over. My three-year hitch in the Army has concluded. Done, finished, back in "the world," the term we used for civilian life while in the military. My "short-timer's calendar" was now filled with all the days ticked off.

Having disembarked from the 707, I was still in my Class A khaki uniform, with its medals, awards, rank (sp/5), and jump wings.

All those belonged to the world from which I was now severed. Now replaced with an Honorable Discharge and a pat on the back.

Soon I'd be on a plane to Detroit and the uniform would go into a closet to become a memory.

Subsequent travels would swallow up even those few mementoes, and soon all that remained would be my jump wings signifying my status as a Paratrooper, and various copies of orders and discharge papers, and a few scattered pictures.

For many years those same jump wings would be kept on a keychain. Miraculously it was an item I never managed to lose or misplace.

Tired of the jump wings wearing a hole in my pocket, I eventually took those jump wings to my local jeweler to see if they had any suggestions as to how it could be made into a bracelet. Looking over some silver chains, the jeweler reconfigured the chain and wings to be soldered to a bracelet.

I wear it to this day.

The GI Bill to pay for my university, my prime motivation for enlisting, was still available, but now no longer held interest. My mind was too scrambled and unfocused to even give it passing consideration.

My previous job at the bank, which was guaranteed to me by law, I let go.

Then 22, I felt old. Those my age around me seemed happy and care-free to a degree I could no longer connect with.

Many years would pass before I was able to identify and relate to my emotions.

The sense of celebration I thought this long-awaited moment would bring, was instead rather the opposite: emptiness, disconnectedness, loss, pain, sadness, heartsickness, a lack of direction, no motivation, anger, and a sense of blown opportunities.

CHAPTER 14:

New York Fashion Week

————◆◆——

Designers

LOOKING AT PICTURES OF TODAY'S TROOPERS—CAMOU-
flage uniforms, body armor, shades, night vision goggles, 30-round clips
verses our 20-round clips—reveals quite a contrast to what we were issued.
Gloves? What, are you kidding me? Cool, lightweight helmets? Nifty foot
attire? Bring on the fashion photographers!

Compare that with our Boonie attire. Our helmet was a pot (heavy,
too!) made of steel, not Kevlar or some other synthetic, wrapped with a
camouflage cloth cover and a helmet linker on the inside of the pot to hold
the whole works together. An elastic camouflage band went around the
outside rim of the helmet, often holding a small bottle of insect repellent,
cigarettes, and a small roll of TP.

The chin strap was clipped to the back of the helmet and never used
by us. Graffiti of some sort or another could often be found written on the
camouflage cover. This type of "being out of uniform," a general term for
any uniform infraction, was not be tolerated in the States or many rear
areas in Vietnam for that matter.

Jungle fatigue pants and jungle boots completed the basic uniform.
Belts were not used, or were made from the shoulder slings from M16s.

Both the shirt and pants had more and larger pockets than the uniforms worn Stateside. The cargo pockets on the pants were extra handy when carrying items like clips or maps.

The jungle boots were a combination of leather and fabric and new on the scene then, different from the all-leather Stateside ones. They would be good for about five to six months if you were lucky. After which they would need replacing.

A long-sleeved woollen (that's right) undershirt that kept us warm at higher elevations in the Central Highlands was much prized. Only worn at night, we took it off to pack away in our bedroll come morning.

When in the rear area, easy ways to distinguish a front-line soldier from a rear-echelon GI were the boots and camouflage cover on the helmet. The front-line Trooper had scuffed boots with the polish long gone. And the front-line Trooper's camouflage cover, a material stretched over the steel pot, was well-bleached and faded by the sun and covered with liberal amounts of graffiti.

The jungle fatigues issued to us had just made it on the scene at the time and were not available to Stateside troops. It was a light material, OD (olive drab) in color, and its claim to fame was its ability to quickly dry by one's body heat if wet. During the monsoon rains, that quality alone made it invaluable.

If it wasn't raining, it might just as well have been. The constant sweat pouring off our bodies was wicked off with these uniforms.

Socks were very important; a couple of extra pairs would go a long way in protecting one's feet. The constant heat and moisture made wet feet a breeding ground for numerous infections, fungus, blisters, and general jungle rot.

Forget your Fruit of the Loom or (insert you brand choice here). We didn't wear any. Why? For many of the same reasons given above, with chafing and jungle rot the most common.

Soft hats (Boonie hats) with a circular brim were popular. I would make it a point to keep frag pins pulled from grenades in firefights hanging around the brim. It was my intention to hang on to it but I lost it in transit at some point.

Rosaries and religious medals were very common, as were necklaces fashioned from '16, '60, or AK rounds. I made mine the standard way, popping the round off the cartridge using another empty casing and tossing the cartridge and gunpowder. Melt the lead interior and insert a wire loop into the bullet and voila! Hang it on a string or chain, that's it.

Dog tags would be taped over to hide the reflective metal and to prevent any clinking sounds.

All rank insignia, name tags, and units patches were usually left off for security reasons. Watches were worn, but usually covered.

Tattoos, though not uncommon, were no way near as prevalent as they are these days.

Piercings? The only ones I saw were made by bullets or other foreign objects violating the body. Yes, we did our piercings the old fashion way!

Another critical item, and not much bigger than a hand cloth: the all-important towel. Yes, a small OD towel that we draped around our necks. Worth its weight in gold. Used to wipe away the constant sweat, and to keep ants, leeches, you name it from dropping down your neck. And to cover your weapon's critical firing mechanism from the swirling dust while boarding and disembarking choppers. It had a number of uses that made it invaluable over the course of a day.

I often felt out of place wearing glasses with not much in the way of styles to select from. Two choices, Buddy Holly Special or standard Nerd, were the only game in town. Contacts were in their infancy, and even if available would be impractical in the Boonies. "Could you please stop shooting at me until I have my contacts in?" Trying to appear a battle-hardened veteran, the image was hard for me to convey since I could get away without shaving in those days. Where's the stubble? And again, I wore glasses.

Heading out to the Boonies we would be seen loaded for bear with Load Bearing Equipment (web belts & suspenders, rucksacks, and full ammo).

CHAPTER 15:

Tanks

———◆——

HERE IS A BIT OF AN ODD STORY ABOUT A MOUNTAIN rising out of a plain by itself in a peculiar way, on top of which sits one of our communications outposts.

It takes place sometime around the Tet Offensive, in the southern part of the country.

So visible, an appealing target in many respects. Sure, it's got its share of defenses. But like all defensive outpost bunkers, the safety of these static emplacements rest at the mercy of the attacker.

It's the attacker who determines when to attack or withdraw. Timing is everything. The weather, the time of day, the element of surprise—these factors are an extra weapon that can be used against the defenders.

It could be an all-out attack or something that continually chips away at the defenders. Mortars, rockets, snipers. Deadly irritants.

And that's where we came in. Our mission was to scour the mountain in hopes of finding and eliminating these NVA. Search and destroy: our specialty, off we go. It didn't appear to be that big a deal.

It was a large mountain, heavily covered with jungle canopy and its share of ravines and uneven terrain. Continual mist and fog made it more unpleasant.

Up and down, round and round we searched for the NVA. With ambushes set, one of our platoons got a couple of NVA.

One detail that stuck out in our many patrols was continually coming across trees with notches cut into them. These notches were blackened by fire.

Very puzzling. It wasn't until discussing this with Sergeant B. many years later that I found out the NVA mortar crews would light candles in the notches at night and use them as "sight lines" for firing on the outpost at the top of the hill.

One particular time when we were near the base of the mountain, dusk was coming on fast. When you're enveloped by heavily foliaged trees with little light visible, fast means fast. Once that sun sets, complete darkness arrives in no time flat.

We had barely stopped to prepare a night perimeter when within a stone's throw, just out of sight, we heard Vietnamese voices and the clanging of pots and pans. We were all taken aback. Haven't those guys ever heard about noise discipline?

We're stunned that the object of our search could be so obliging as to announce their presence to us in this dramatic fashion.

Not a peep from us, all holding our breath, as we make preparations to attack. But Mother Nature has other plans, light is dimming quickly, and it is decided a morning attack would be more prudent.

The surrounding bush was very thick. Even with our initial surprise, it was difficult to see how any noise made as we approached them would not lead to them responding with the first shots and us taking the first casualties.

We continued to hear the Vietnamese talk among themselves, still apparently unaware of our presence.

So far, so good; that's how we intended to keep it.

With the complete darkness of night upon us, maintaining noise discipline and waiting for dawn is all that remained for us to do.

Now there are certain critters, birds and rats to name a few, whose travel through the bush mimics the sound of approaching people. Just the amount of rustling, then pausing, rustling, and pausing. It is unnerving if you don't know better.

I knew better, but tell that to S******. A nice guy, but during a similar situation, he proved to have a jumpy trigger finger.

He did it again. He fired. (The noise!)

As I said earlier in the book, firing one's weapon at night without a body to show for it is a cardinal sin.

The cat's out of the bag, our cover is blown. Our element of surprise is gone. Once potential ambushers, we're the ones in deep s**t now.

Morning dawns and we're all on edge. There is no way we'll be able to move on them without being hit first, a very unappealing prospect. But fate intervenes again.

Not that far away, intense firing breaks out. The volume of fire indicates not just small arms but heavier weapons: one of our armored units is being hit.

I hear bits and pieces of radio chatter, with the always out-of-sync firing over the radio, with the actual firing being heard live seconds later.

We are requested to go to their aid.

Our move to attack the enemy "pots and pans outfit" is put aside.

Away we go towards the main action taking place further away. The closer we get, the less firing we hear. Whether it's our superior force or whatever, the NVA break off contact before we arrive. That's fine with me.

It was the 17th Cavalry that we had come to aid. The excitement subsided, I was able to take in our new buddies in the armored outfit. It was the only occasion of being together in combat. The mountains and terrain that were our normal AO could not accommodate all this fine firepower.

Tank crews were telling me their woes of the turret mechanism on their tank being busted and how they've been having to use the manual mode, which I imagined to be a big hand crank. Yes, even the wheels of war have to be kept oiled and working. The routine and mundane must be attended to, or the other side will kill you because they are better at their routines.

Beyond that, I'm struck by all the cases of beer they have secured encircling the turret. Talk about drinking and driving.

This would be our only interaction working with an armored unit. It was only for a day or so, and then we moved on.

I don't know how good they were, but that whole beer-around-the-turret thing didn't strike me as good military discipline. Then again, having a few beers and firing off that cannon or .50 caliber—what could be more fun!

As Z****, one of my platoon buddies, reminded me, they seemed to be out of a scene from that old war movie, *Kelly's Heroes.*

If the truth be told, much more of that blend of bizarre reality exists than will ever be admitted to. Most can only be found in a war zone setting and never sees the light of day.

Some of these events are found in the larger-than-life personalities of individuals or the weird interaction of events.

CHAPTER 16:

FAG

THERE "IT" IS AND THERE "*IT*" IS.

The first "it" being the exit for my home trucking terminal in Joplin, Missouri, where I'll refuel and take a well-needed break after leaving Dallas, Texas earlier in the day before continuing on to Toronto, Canada.

The second "it" are the larger-than-life letters "FAG" on a nearby office building, at that same exit. They get a lot of comments from truckers on their CBs who pass it and don't know what it means.

FAG is the acronym for Fischer Aktien-Gesellschaft, one of the oldest and largest German ball-bearing companies in the world. I've seen that company name on billboards, buildings, and magazines, and those in the steel industry are well-acquainted with its meaning. In fact, FAG pretty well invented and patented the first steel ball bearings and they have been in business for over 100 years.

Words contain a lot of power. Depending on their context, the part of the world they're used in, and the generation using or hearing them, their meaning can change and how they're used or misused can get you in a lot of trouble. Those three simple letters could still get you killed in certain parts of the world.

If you use or hear the word "fag" in England and Australia, they're most likely talking about cigarettes, as it's common slang for cigarettes.

Here in North America, "fag" is known as a slur against homosexuals, and it's the meaning that initially comes to mind when the word is used here.

When I was younger, say the word "gay" and everyone assumed you meant happy and lighthearted. A few generations later, say the same word "gay" and the predominant meaning is homosexual.

I say that to illustrate how within one's lifetime, a single word can totally change how it's understood and perceived in a culture or country.

So, the same word and you get three totally different meanings in three different parts of the world.

Phan Rang, Vietnam is midway down the coast of South Vietnam on the South China Sea. By all accounts, Phan Rang was one of the safest rear areas during the war. Our company had returned from Chu Lai in the north and was on Stand Down for four days before heading out on the next search-and-destroy operation.

Stand Down was a three to four day break from our month in the Boonies, usually at a main base camp in the heavily fortified rear area.

In addition to being the home base for the First Brigade, 101st Airborne, the airbase was also home to a squadron of Canberra bombers from Australia, one of our allies at the time, and a division of South Korean Marines.

The security for the airfield perimeter was provided by their own troops, a contingent of security police.

Of course their troops had different uniforms than us, and big on the "cool" factor was their headgear. They had those safari-like bush hats with the flap folded up and pinned to one side. I had to get me one.

My friend Sergeant D. and myself linked up with an Aussie soldier and were hanging out in search of someplace different to eat. With weapons left behind in the squad tents and not even a knife on me, we wandered towards the airfield in search of a canteen that we heard served burgers (good luck with that!).

We located a canteen that served what they claimed were burgers. We weren't impressed. Still, it was a place to hang out and shoot the breeze with our newfound Australian buddy. He belonged to an Air Force unit that was in charge of patrolling the perimeter of the Air Base. I remember him being a mild-mannered, nice guy who certainly didn't seem to be a threat to anyone.

My friend Sergeant D. also came across as a nice guy, but had an awesome reputation in a firefight, something you couldn't tell by looking at him.

The three of us took a seat on an arrangement of picnic tables outside. Part of my new buddy's uniform was that traditional bush hat as his head gear. Imagine a big game hunter with the hat brim pinned up and a cool headband. We began talking about our Aussie buddy's cool bush hat and how I coveted it. My Aussie friend in turn thought we had cool weapons, in particular, fragmentation grenades that weren't issued to them, and how he wished he had some.

We in turn got all the "frags" we wanted, as many as we could carry.

It didn't take much haggling before my new Aussie friend agreed to a trade, a cool Aussie bush hat for me, a few frags for him. Done. We arranged a transfer for the following day.

About this time a dozen or so black dudes wander in, talking trash among themselves. I instantly peg them as "Boonie rats" by their boots and uniforms, but don't recognize them as from our company. Some of them seem to have an attitude, but we stick to ourselves and mind our own business.

They do likewise. These were the days of the Black Power movement, with a strong assertion of rights for blacks, and lots of these dudes had a chip on their shoulders, rightly or wrongly.

Anyways, among the three of us, our conversation turned to Aborigines in Australia. Our Aussie buddy kept referring to the Aborigines as "blacks," the term used by Australians in general. At the time, that was not a common word in the American lexicon when talking about the "black" community; if anything, it carried a negative connotation.

Our Aussie friend also told us how they called cigarettes "fags" and he went on telling us how he liked American "fags."

So if you're seated at the black dudes' table, most of the words coming from the Aussie's mouth sounded like this: Black, fags, black, fags, blacks, fags.

Bam!

Out of the blue, with a classic sucker-punch, one of the black Troopers seated at a picnic table beside us hit our Aussie buddy in the face and knocked him out cold. He slumped face-forward onto our table.

What the f**k! None of us three saw it coming. We hadn't even been talking with them, let alone about them.

Sergeant D. and me jump up to face off with these dozen or so black dudes. Knives are pulled—a great reminder of why they don't let everyone walk around the rear area with a '16 in one hand and a beer in the other. Words are exchanged but it doesn't go beyond that.

The totally lopsided odds and cooler heads prevented the whole scene from getting really ugly. Being cut and stabbed will get you killed just as well as a bullet. If the odds hadn't been 4:1 against us, that very well might have happened.

Our Aussie buddy came to and recovered after about a minute, wondering what hit him. I told him some people took offense to his use of the words "blacks" and "fags," and not knowing the context, slugged him. Hard to believe, but at that time, being called "black" rather than "negro" was a big insult.

Putting this unfortunate mishap behind us, we agreed to meet the next day to complete the "bush hat" and frag swap.

Never happened. Our Stand Down was cut short, and with little notice we were choppered out to the Boonies a day early. Darn! Having that Aussie bush hat would have been a cool addition to my wardrobe.

It's one of those events where I wish I could've made note of the Aussie's name and unit and later linked up to reminisce. Who knows, might still happen?

CHAPTER 17:

Duds

—————————◆—————————

DUDS: SHELLS, BOMBS, MISSILES, EXPLOSIVES THAT FAIL
to go off when fired.

The police are at your door and telling you that you've got to evacuate the premises immediately. Grab your dog and cat and let's go. Now.

An unexploded 500-pound bomb has been uncovered at a construction site less than a block away. Until the bomb squad disposes of it,
nobody in the area is safe.

I read that article recently and my attention perked up, knowing
what could be involved.

Ongoing stories like the above are found on back pages of newspapers or on news feeds. Most stories like this go unnoticed.

That particular incident took place in England.

To this day, farmers uncover mustard and chlorine gas shells from as
far back as World War I, along with high-explosive shells. Many are unstable and continue to cause injury and death. This "harvest of steel" continues more than 100 years since they were planted.

In World War II, many bombs dropped by planes had a variety of
delayed-action fuses that didn't trigger as intended and await the slightest
movement to renew their deadly intent. Others simply malfunctioned.

Also from World War II, large sections of North African desert
remain off limits because of minefields. These contain everything from

anti-tank to anti-personnel mines waiting to blow your camel sky high. Many parts of sub-Saharan Africa in recent and ongoing conflicts are littered with mines that are killing and maiming present and future generations. Although these areas are supposed to be mapped out, even if records are made, with the chaos of war they get lost or fade into the files of time. Huge areas of real estate in the Middle East, Southeast Asia, parts of Eastern Europe (Ukraine, anyone?), and Africa remain places you want to avoid.

Less so, but even here in the United States, bombing and artillery ranges are littered with a percentage of duds. Off the beaten track, these vast acres are classified and won't show up on realtors' websites anytime soon. Cluster bombs, which are bombs within bombs, contain delay fuses. Kids, the most unsuspecting, are those that suffer the greatest, losing life or limb. They often pick them up, thinking them to be toys of some sort, and bam!

Armed with metal detectors of all descriptions, an industry of bomb-disposal experts ("expert" is a relative concept in that business) follow behind these wars in an attempt to contain all of that ordinance. Their task is overwhelming, and as can be guessed, it is not a job everyone at the local unemployment office is eager to sign up for. It's a specialty job requiring nerves of steel that only few are cut out for.

High in the mountains off Da Nang, pausing for a break, I noticed a metallic glint of an object by a boulder I'd been leaning up against.

What do we have here? Oh, a dud artillery shell, wedged between some rocks. I casually get our CE (combat engineer) to see what to do about it. Normally we'd explode it in place, but in this case we let it be so as to not reveal our location.

As a rule these duds are destroyed, since the VC would often dismantle and reconfigure the explosives to be used against us, in the form of a booby trap. This was done throughout the war. We can only guess how many of our own weapons later boomeranged back at us.

Sometimes we were our own enemy. Faulty fragmentation grenades. I always kept an eye on the pin/blasting cap that could come unscrewed from the frag, leaving an exposed blasting cap with the frag having dropped off somewhere. A variation of this resulted in one of our guys losing his hand. That word "dud" begins to sound less innocent by now.

All the unexploded artillery rounds that landed in the Perfume River near Hue, are just waiting for an unsuspecting fisherman or construction project to resume their journey of death initiated 50 years earlier.

A wounded Marine is rushed into a field ER. Lodged in his torso: an unexploded RPG round or '79 round from the NVA. Freaked-out medical staff are scrambling to find a way to save a life without losing theirs in the process. Less common, thank God, yet not unheard of.

During World War I, chemical warfare made its nightmarish debut just over 100 years ago. Originally used by the Germans, the chemist who came up with the idea thought it would shorten the war and in that respect, considered it to be a more humane weapon.

Primarily chlorine and mustard gas, eventually chemical weapons were used on a massive scale by both sides. So horrific were the results that when World War II rolled around, there was a tacit agreement not to use them.

Like all munitions, these weapons have a shelf-life, and even if never used still present problems as to disposal. An expense that countries don't budget for, the bill does come due though.

CS gas was military-grade tear gas. We kept the odd CS grenade around, mostly used in tunnels in Vietnam.

Playing "war games" back in the United States, one was tossed in my direction. Hey, I'll toss it back. Reaching to grab it, the wind shifted and I inhaled a mouthful of CS gas as it billowed out of the canister. I thought my lungs were going to drop out. In damp, misty air it clings to the skin, leaving a burning sensation.

Nasty stuff, just so you know if planning on joining a riot of one type or another.

Nerve gas, more of the same, and dare I say, the worst! Stockpiles exist. Same problems: shelf life, disposal. Raise your hand if you want to help taking this stuff to the proverbial trash dump.

Different varieties exist, all horrific.

Biological warfare, of course, represents more mayhem.

Chicago to LA. Good miles, goes my thinking. With the snow flying, I'll take the southern route, which will take me through some of my favorite parts of the Southwest.

Once I hit Santa Rosa, New Mexico, I get off the "big road" and pick up Highway 54 and head due south. The traffic of the interstate drops off dramatically, and the high desert will slowly descend through some of my favorite desert towns: Vaughn, Corona, Carrizoza, Tularosa, and then Alamogordo.

On July 16, 1945, the world's first atomic bomb was exploded in this area. It is the test site for the Pandora's box of death that would soon be used on Japan.

Any weapon that vaporizes more than 100,000 human beings in less time than it takes to write this paragraph gives pause for thought, not to mention the countless survivors left to slow and agonizing suffering.

The names of those killed by that bomb would fill the equivalent of two Vietnamese Wall Memorials, a monument that took more than 15 years to fill. That knowledge always drifts through my head anytime I pass this way. The place where Pandora's box was opened.

And yet it remains a scenic spot, with beautiful, colorful mountain ranges surrounding the area.

It's at Alamogordo that I pick up Highway 70 and cut east towards Las Cruces, New Mexico. And will then continue on to LA.

But not just yet.

Highway 70 is having one of its temporary shutdowns as the White Sands Missile Range conducts one of its classified tests. An hour goes by before the road is finally reopened by the Military Police.

I resume my journey, admiring the white sand dunes that keep trying to drift onto the road.

So much beauty side-by-side with the tools of war.

Nuclear weapons. Yes, here we do have worse.

On at least one occasion, duds of these weapons lie under the ocean floor from a bomber incident gone south.

Yes, these also have shelf-life, and the costs on all levels to build, maintain, and dispose of these guys boggles the mind.

Having lived through a Cold War, I can't believe all that insanity is now making a comeback. Coincidentally, my morning news feed reads "Nuclear Poker."

Not an activity you want to be "bluffing" with.

CHAPTER 18:

Montana

---◆---

Tombstones

LOCATED NEAR THE HILLS OF LITTLE BIG HORN, Montana lie markers for the U.S. Cavalry soldiers who were wiped out doing battle with the Sioux Indians.

We all know the main participants here: U.S. General Custer for the Cavalry, and Sitting Bull and Crazy Horse for the Sioux. The individual participants from both sides, many of whom no doubt displayed great courage, are lost to us, with nobody there to record their deeds.

As a former soldier in the U.S. Army, I identify with all participants.

Gen. Custer, whose hometown is just forty miles south of me in Monroe, Michigan.

Sitting Bull and the Native Americans (as the T-shirts read, "the Original Homeland Security"), who were fighting to maintain their lands and culture, also have my sympathy.

About 101 miles away (101st Airborne—strange coincidence?) from Little Bighorn in Montana lies the small town of Rosebud, Montana, just off from Interstate I-94. The countryside in this part of Montana is more open, with lots of grassland.

I prefer the parts of Montana farther west, by Livingston or Three Forks. Farther west still, closer to the Idaho border, the mountains grow larger, darker, and steeper—memories of 'Nam creep in.

Rosebud, Little Big Horn—I had trucked by both places many times, but with a 53-foot trailer and the added length of my Kenworth tractor, parking was always an issue and prevented me from stopping to pay respects to Sergeant D. in particular. My tight "just-in-time" delivery schedules left little fat in my day. It would have to wait, if it ever happened at all.

In the cemeteries lies the tombstone of Sgt. D., linked as we were by combat, hanging out in Phan Rang and generally shooting the breeze when our paths crossed in those days.

I was in the Third Platoon Charlie Company, and Sergeant D. in the Second, both of us in Charlie Company.

He had a reputation as a good fighter and definitely a person to have on your side when the "s**t hits the fan." Given all the surrounding chaos and confusion in jungle combat, it's important to know that everyone is playing their part. D. would be doing that, and more.

We were pushing our way into the A Shau Valley. No Allied presence there since the French left twenty years prior. A big-time NVA infiltration point and they've been having the run of the place all that time. Extensive bunkers, tunnels, trails, and even roads crisscrossed the area.

The 101st Airborne went there to put an end to that. We were all combat vets by then and had no illusion of what we would be facing.

Morning, I was still wrapped up in my pancho liner, peeking at my '16 on its bi-pod, ready to go. The first hint of light had my Platoon Sergeant quietly come to me, whispering, "Gooks at the perimeter" (less than 100 feet away).

No sooner than I secure my bedroll, and not having time for breakfast, I hear automatic-weapon fire. Sergeant P. in our platoon opened up and hit two NVA who were probing our perimeter. The NVA pulled their dead/wounded back. *Here we go again*, I thought, but at least we got in the first shots.

Similar to encounters earlier that week, each time ending with fewer of us, even with our 10 to 1 kill ratio, it's small consolation to know many more NVA await entrenched in bunkers up the trail, and it's up the trail we're heading.

So began another firefight, typical yet each was unique in its own way. The quiet, alternating with the intense noise of automatic weapons, explosions, yelling for medics, and insane amounts of rounds and tracers going in every direction. Minutes, and then hours passed, with progress in mere yards. Yet insane as it seems, we have to push forward and destroy them.

The RPD machine gun had been chewing up the tree that I was using for cover. The tree wasn't big enough for me. Tracers/rounds from the RPD came from a bunker less than 50 yards to my front. He was raking the area directly over my head. Firing bursts, a pause, more busts, another pause, leaves and twigs come fluttering down on me. More bursts, I'm sucking myself into the ground and working on more ways to make myself flatter, more rounds coming my way, more leaves and twigs landing on me. No, I'm not about to stick my head up until he slacks off. He's got the 100-round canister drum and me with a 20-round clip.

Some explosions, frags, LAWs, RPG. The firing finally eases off. It reaches the point where I could plan how to move forward. One of our guys took out the bunker with a LAW. But not before we took more casualties from a RPG.

Sgt D. appears in my view between me and the bunker, crouched low and circling around in some type of flanking maneuver, alone.

He pauses momentarily. Our eyes meet, but he is totally focused and his eyes communicate nothing to me. He continues on his way.

I was struck by his seeming lack of ammo, just his '16. Not even carrying a bandolier of backup clips? That told me he was almost out of ammo. Yet here he was risking being caught in the open. At this stage of the game, every shot fired has a lot of thought behind it, each one has to count! I still had a decent amount of ammo and would have joined him in whatever he was up to if he gave the least indication. I felt bad, a couple months before, Sergeant D., one of my best friends, ceased communicating with me. Why?

He moved on, completely focused/committed to his one-man assault in our sector of the firefight.

Finally, and none too soon, the Gunships arrived.

If you caught yourself anywhere close to where they were laying down their fire, it would immediately be clear why they have such a fearsome reputation. A flying weapons platform, providing maximum firepower was their sole mission. And they did it well.

Dual Gatling mini-machine guns, each firing 6,000 rounds a minute. To hear them firing sounds like the buzz-saw of death that the Gunship is. Rocket pods on each side packed both with high-explosive rockets and white phosphorus (Willie Peter) rockets. Whether it's the Huey Gunship or the newer Cobra Gunship, they're equally deadly. The whoosh of the rockets firing, closely followed by the tremendous explosions of the rockets slamming into the earth close by—all that will soon be coming.

We pop a red-smoke grenade—red to mark our position— and radio to the choppers about where to lay down their munitions. Hoping some of those rockets find their way into the bunkers that have been giving us all that trouble.

It was time for us to get behind the biggest tree or whatever cover was available, hunker down the best we could, and let the Gunships do their work.

And they did it well, they devastated the area. Then they back off and we are able to finally advance and knock out the bunkers without too much effort. About f**kin' time!

It sticks in my mind how well constructed those NVA bunkers were. The interior earth walls smooth, low to the ground, the machine guns slits between logs almost invisible.

How concealed....

That glance that passed between us was my final vision of Sergeant D. Later, from others, I heard he helped knock out bunker(s). The dead NVA were no longer an issue.

I came through that day without being hit, but others in my platoon were not so lucky. By now I'm one of the few not having been wounded and I knew this luck couldn't last much longer. I was into the seventh month of my twelve-month tour, and the odds weren't in my favor. Just making it through a week has become an ordeal. The whole area is crawling with NVA.

Gathered on the LZ awaiting the choppers to take away our wounded, no KIAs (killed in actions) on our side, thank God. Dead NVA lay around, in bunkers, on trails. We gathered up captured weapons (AKs, SKS, RPGs, RPDs) .Maybe some trophies from the dead bodies.

There's a brief period after a firefight like this when I have this feeling of euphoria. I'm alive, they're dead. We won, they lost.

I know it won't last. Still, I savor it while I can.

Our resupply choppers come swooping in, tossing out fresh ammo.

Sergeant G. Hops out. "Hi guys," he says with a big smile on his face. A valued veteran of our platoon. His cheerfulness was a huge contrast to the bodies lying around us. He had been back in the States for an emergency family medical leave.

Then I hear my name called out. I was told to get on the next chopper; my orders had arrived. It couldn't have been at a better or the worst time. I survived yet another firefight, but leaving friends behind without goodbyes Top (Sergeant) and myself grabbed a poncho load of captured weapons and threw them in the chopper, and then hopped on.

The chopper slowly lifted off. I could hear some AK rounds cracking close to us above the noise of the rotor blades. A parting farewell from NVA lurking in the area. A fellow Trooper with me flinched when hearing the AK. My ears were super fine tuned to weapons fire. I recall thinking, *Not to worry, those rounds are feet away, not inches, no need to duck.*

I was relieved that I was leaving all that death and fear, but bummed that it should be in this manner, with some friends remaining below.

A month or so earlier I had elected to use my "get out of jail free" card. I like to see things through, and leaving in this manner was not my desire. This I obtained in December 1967; it was now March 31, 1968.

A week or two after that firefight, I was at our rear base camp. Looking for a cold drink, I enter our EM (enlisted men's) club. Basically a one-room building with some tables, chairs, and music. A bar of sorts serving cheap, warm, off-brand beer and some pop.

Walking through the door, in the first sounds I hear is the hit song "Sitting by the Dock of the Bay" by Otis Redding. One of my all-time favorites. That music connection was to change shortly.

Spotting some guys from our company but not in my platoon, I walk over to see what's up and why they're not in the Boonies.

"We're here to escort the body of my friend, Sergeant D., of the second platoon, back to the States," they tell me. He was killed with small arms this past week.

I was stunned. One of our company's best fighters, he had been a good friend. Despite all he'd been through, you had the feeling he would survive his tour.

He took a burst of automatic fire and was killed outright. The A Shau Valley claimed one of our best. I was in shock. From then on that Otis Redding song remains forever linked to D.'s death.

About a week after that, our CO, Captain A., was killed in a similar manner by an AK burst to the chest. In a freak choice of events he mistakenly took the wrong fork in a trail only to run into an NVA soldier.

The jungle receded, but not so the memory of the events and friendships of those days. Survivor's guilt remains over friends left behind, both who died there and some whom I've met years later at our reunions.

I was on my way to the rear. There I would awaiting orders for what ended up being Okinawa, my next duty station.

It was to be another 25 years before one of my squad leaders (Sergeant P.) tracked me down, leading to a slow reconnection with surviving members of my company at various reunions.

One of these reconnections was as recent as this past month, July/2018. A.G. (in my platoon) and I talked on the phone. More pieces of the puzzle are filled in. He sent me a picture of him and my buddy A.P., now dead. It is a great picture and in relatively good condition given its age.

CHAPTER 19:
Hot LZ

———◆◆———

I WAS BEATING THE GROUND TO DEATH WITH MY entrenching tool, a shovel, and making zero progress. In rapid succession, more "slicks" were swooping in around me as the rest of Charlie Company got off to do the same.

Our company had been pulled out of the Boonies to the west of Hue to join the fight and encircle an NVA base camp that lay below me by the Perfume River.

I tried the pick side of my entrenching tool; no luck there either. The ground was mostly shale rock, providing me with nothing but frustration, motivated as I was to dig a deep hole to escape the fate met by our two dead Recon troops in the valley to my right.

Killed with a .51-caliber machine gun. It's always said that rounds from a machine gun that size will go through a concrete block and it'll just make it mad. More than kill, it mutilates.

The hill I was on contained little cover and was not that high, yet it did give me a commanding view of the action below. However, being fully exposed and in view of the NVA below was not reassuring. I was in easy range of that .51-caliber. I resumed my digging.

I remember noting a larger-than-life size religious statue off to my right near the summit of the same hill I was on. It seemed out of place with all the violence taking place.

Nearing the bottom of the hill, along the river bank, the vegetation became very thick and nothing could be seen. Somewhere in there was a battalion-sized NVA base camp. To my right, having descended into the valley, one of our platoons was making its way to link up with the pinned-down members of the Recon unit. With great risk to their own lives, the platoon managed to retrieve our dead, without taking further casualties.

Also in the valley but to my left, Alpha Company had set up a blocking force and was heavily engaged with the NVA.

So, we had them surrounded. Charlie Company (me) on the hill. Recon and one of our platoons on the right. Alpha Company on my left. What about the fourth side?

The Perfume River took care of that. We were downriver from the old Imperial capital of Hue, the scene of ferocious fighting during the recent Tet Offensive.

We had them boxed in.

A period of time passed and, with the recognition that nothing was being fired my way, I eased my efforts to dig the unyielding shale and surveyed the scene below.

With good reason the NVA weren't sticking their heads out: A pair of F4s (jets) had made their entrance.

With their approach just above treetop level and from my right, parallel to the river, they began multiple passes, dropping 250-pound bombs while strafing with their 20-mm cannons. A sight to see!

They would pull up, circle back, and then repeat the process. The explosions from the bombs, the buzz-saw of the 20-mm's. This was done a few times until their ordinance was spent.

My fear of taking fire from below lessened given the firepower being brought to bear on the NVA.

We were maintaining our blocking position on the hill and I was feeling more like a spectator than a participant at this stage. With front-row bleacher seats, if you will, right on the 50-yard line.

The jets had done their thing, but it was only the beginning, setting the stage for the next part: Gunships. Choppers with 6,000 round/minute mini-guns and rockets pods packed with HE and Willie Peter rockets. They took over where the jets left off, approaching from the same direction.

They started laying down fire. Much feared and for good reason, they did their work without response from below.

Their slow, circling passes contrasted with the extreme speed their rockets made slamming into the ground. The buzzing sound of the mini-guns that could cover an area of a football field in seconds.

Eventually they too expended their ordnance and left the scene. Having waited their turn, miles away in the rear area, more firepower is brought to bear, the Artillery. 155s, 175s—the big guns. With the aircraft out of the way, they began their job. With long-range capabilities, we were well within their reach. Again from the right the rounds came screaming and whistling in. Exploding black bursts marked their impact and were very visible from my "bleacher" seat.

In that barrage of artillery fire I noticed a number of duds, unexploded rounds, hit the river. Not sure why that was—angle of trajectory, water surface? Twenty percent duds, but for the rounds that exploded, the accuracy was there and that's what counted.

With those three coatings of death rained on them, it now remained for us to go in there and finish the job. Not a welcome thought because despite the pounding they received, this is the land of tunnels. We had to approach with caution knowing they could have weathered the storm and be laying for us.

Mother Nature intervened with falling light. Our final assault would have to wait until morning.

Night passed without any activity in our sector.

Not the same with Alpha Company. They had more activity with NVA attempting to break out along the river through their sector. They suffered KIAs and WIAs.

At first light we ate and readied ourselves for the push into the valley. Rucksacks were left and all available ammo was removed and piled on and around our bodies. Bandoliers of '16 clips, many 100-round links of '60 ammo crisscrossed our bodies. Frags were double-checked and made handy.

The encounter proved anticlimactic. Leaving behind some medical staff (we later transported them to the rear for interrogation) to care for the most severely wounded, and a few bodies floating in the river, but other than that, they were gone. The NVA wisely chose to make their get-away overnight. A few parting shots from across the river, but nothing of consequence.

The choppers came and returned us to the Boonies. Back to the same AO we had been plucked from the day before. Many NVA yet to be discovered remained there.

My past fears, which would wax and wane, now began to settle on me more like the morning fog and mist seen in the valleys. Unlike the mist, they would not dissolve with the rising sun. There was no such sun to dissolve the feelings building in me. Three or four factors had been grating and were affecting my state of mind.

A decision that I never considered making had now coming into view as a possibility.

Time to use my "get out of jail" card.

Brian.

CHAPTER 20:

Top Chef 3

———————◆▸◂———————

IN ADDITION TO A CASE OF C-RATIONS WE EACH
received a mixed assortment of goodies that fell under the general heading
of "sundries." Some of these items are as follows.

"Heating tabs" (large solid-fuel tablets to heat our C-rations), coffee,
hot chocolate, halazone tablets for water purification, malaria pills.

Clothing. For those of us whose jungle fatigues had become too badly
torn (the pants normally got the worst of it), a batch of jungle fatigues was
sent out on a resupply chopper. They would be tossed out and it's left up to
you to dive in, first come, first served. The discarded clothing would end
up in the firepit.

Very important to me then, my carton of cigarettes, Winstons my
first choice, or Marlboro. I was a two to three packs a day smoker at the
time. I managed to quit 10 or so years later. Most of us smoked, and in
hindsight it's harmful to one's health in ways we are all aware of now, but
also to nonsmokers, the odor of cigarettes travels a long way and alerts
them to our presence. I didn't realize how far that smell permeated everything and it would no doubt give the unseen enemy a leg up on our whereabouts, the cigarette odor announcing our presence.

"Coffin nails" (cigarettes) in small packs of four also came within
individual C-ration meals. They were without doubt the stalest cigarettes
in the world.

Insect repellent (DEET) in small plastic bottles, plenty of those. A critical item, I would make sure to have plenty on hand.

Various types of candy. I only remember some kind of soft gumdrop candies and "tropical chocolate" bars. The later had the consistency, texture, and taste of chalk. The manufacturer sucked the "chocolate" out to preserve the "tropical." Still, though most of our guys wouldn't take them, I did, to the detriment of my dental hygiene.

Dental hygiene was lacking and overlooked by many. Water being at a premium, not much effort was made to use it in brushing. My toothbrush was a little funky also, as it made a perfect Petri dish for fungus, bacteria and god knows what else.

Brown Bag…it's a hot meal.

Mail Call, a much anticipated part of the resupply process.

Communication was painfully slow. Letters and replies to letters seemed to take forever.

Mail was our only and very limited contact with loved ones back home. Remember, those were the days of snail mail. Our mail was addressed to a general APO (Army post office) in San Francisco and made its way to us in due time. We did the reverse in turn. Larger "Care" packages were held for us in the rear and were obtained once the operation was over. Only on one occasion were packages ever brought to the field.

My parents split up after high school, putting the rest of my family in disarray. Sadly, with no love lost between my father and myself, he went on to work and travel throughout the world. He eventually remarried, and settled and died in Germany in 1986.

Speaking of smoking, there's such a thing as "smokin' a frag." (Don't you kids try this at home.) The following is something I don't relate often, lest people think I'm BS-ing.

"Hey Cherry, Sergeant F. makes you 'smoke a frag' in this platoon."

This was told to me (Cherry) shortly after joining my company in the field as a new replacement.

A new type of cigarettes?? No, it's a procedure to prevent fragmentation grenades from being tossed back out at us once thrown into a tunnel/bunker.

Basically it goes like this. The pin on a fragmentation grenade is pulled, allowing for the handle to fly off, which in turn activates a countdown timer to detonation (about 4 seconds). In training, you're taught (for good reason) to toss that frag immediately after letting the handle fly.

By "smoking a frag," you let the pin fly, and continue holding it in your hand, and then toss it into a tunnel/bunker just prior to explosion. The concept being whoever's inside won't have time to toss it back your way.

This was SOP (standard operating procedure) within our platoon

I almost seriously wounded one of our own doing this. Tossing my "frag" into a tunnel (which had a 90-degree bend inside), it exploded almost immediately. The backblast turned the tunnel entrance into a massive shotgun as shrapnel, rocks, and dirt came flying out.

This came close to blowing away a Trooper near me, who had moved up unaware of my action. No yelling "fire in the hole" in firefights.

Two Resupply Incidents

Ask almost anyone who hangs around aircraft, fixed wing or otherwise, and most will agree that choppers are tricky critters to fly.

There's a lot going on and it's not something you just pop into gear and away you go. Even a good fixed-wing pilot will readily admit to not being able to fly one or even wanting to attempt it.

We had an unusual resupply going on with the company given the fact that we were spread on two different hills, within visual distance of each other, with the resupply choppers handling both simultaneously.

Taxi Anyone?

Sergeant F. decided to make a social call to a fellow Trooper located on the other resupply hill. No need to call a taxi, just climb into one of the many resupply choppers making the rounds. Yes, you can do that type of thing if you have enough rank.

A few hundred yards away, the other hilltop was visible, busy with activity of choppers flying in and out ferrying C-rations.

That chopper looks awfully packed, I remember thinking as Sgt. F. climbed on.

Heat, altitude , and especially weight are some of the critical factors that affect lift capability and must be taken into consideration flying any aircraft, but more so with choppers.

Off they go. Midway between the two hills we notice Sergeant F.'s chopper losing altitude fast. Suddenly, multiple C-ration cases go flying out of the chopper from both sides (doors are always open) in a desperate move to allow the pilot to regain control. The engine had cut out and the pilot had gone into "autorotation" mode. This is essentially an emergency procedure that allows the chopper blades to continue rotating from the weight of the "falling" chopper. Not a pleasant scenario.

With a good skilled pilot, landing hard but safe is achievable. With a pilot not so skilled, broken bones or death result.

Whew! Sgt. F. had a good, skilled pilot. It was a hard landing, with bruises, but everyone survived and lifted off with their now much-reduced weight.

He would have been a big loss to our platoon. Already highly decorated with a Distinguished Service Cross for Valor (he had been put in for a Medal of Honor!), he lived to continue his military career.

Not realizing the seriousness of the situation, those of us watching the incident didn't lose this chance to get in some black humor. We joked that we could see our fellow Troopers on the other hill crying crocodile tears over the loss of some of their Cs that went sailing through the air. No doubt they had to "ration" their remaining C-rations to some degree. A bit of excitement on an otherwise routine resupply.

"X" Marks the Spot

Lots of "chatter" on the radio, an indication that something's up. What's going on this time?

Far from us, but not too far if we really hurry, some NVA soldiers have been spotted. Sergeant F. determines that if we really boot it, we can intersect their path and ambush them.

Leaving rucksacks (and the Cs inside) with the company, and taking all our ammo, off we go.

The pace of travel was the fastest we've ever done. We make our way as quickly as the "wait-a-minute" vines permitted. This pace would've been impossible with our rucksacks, and we were just making it as it is. Not only fast, but we had to go far.

It was the speed and distance together of this venture/trek that made it unique. I wasn't the one with the maps, but man, we were motoring.

Given our rapid rate of travel, I was concerned we might trip a booby trap or ourselves get ambushed.

Exhausted, tired, and a very long distance from our starting point, we prepared an ambush. Skunked, the NVA didn't oblige us, leaving us with another problem—no food.

A decision was made to fly in some Cs.

The terrain we found ourselves in was thick with undergrowth and covered by tall trees. We located a spot that gave us the best chance of the choppers securing an approach and tossing out the C-rations.

It was covered in what looked like banana trees but without any bananas. Hacking away with machetes, it was a pleasant surprise to see how easy it was to slice through these plants. It took no effort—even a dull bayonet could do the job. A better LZ with less work couldn't have been chosen.

Excellent progress was made and before long we had an acceptable-looking LZ. Bring on the choppers.

We could hear them on their approach. Yellow smoke was popped to indicate our location. They should come into view any minute. Where are they?

They radioed that they threw out the Cs at a spot where yellow smoke was rising through the trees.

Apparently the yellow smoke drifted laterally and rose up through the trees at a different location a few hundred feet away. Thinking that was the location, the Cs were chucked out, but from a height of over 100 feet!

Leaving our beautiful LZ, we fought heavy undergrowth to find busted and smashed C-ration cases scattered all over. We ended up making do with what we could find. Many cans were busted open, and now crawling with ants who welcomed this change in their diet.

Bad Karma coming back to us from the chuckle we had at the misfortune of that other resupply gone wrong?

CHAPTER 21:

All God's Creatures, from Ants to Elephants

———————◆◀▬———————

Phan Rang

SHORTLY AFTER ARRIVING "IN COUNTRY," I WAS SENT TO Phan Rang, the main base camp for the First Brigade of the 101st Airborne Division (which was later relocated to Bien Hoa).

My company, Charlie Company C, 2/502, was involved in heavy combat further north in the Chu Lai area. Within a week I would be up there joining them. Until then, I was making myself familiar with my local surroundings.

Hmmm, what do we have here? Yes, it is a reptile zoo on our base, including cobras. I'm not referring to the Cobra gunship attack helicopter. I'm talking about the ones with the hoods—the snakes. Highly poisonous and common in Vietnam, along with many other vipers.

Interestingly, it kind of sets the stage as to what I'm in for once I hit the Boonies. I think I'll ask the medic if they issue any anti-venom serum. They don't.

We are issued malaria pills. These have to be taken daily, the small ones six days a week and a big one on Mondays. These are only about 75% effective against malaria.

Carried by mosquitoes, malaria is by far the bigger danger and threat than a viper bite. Close to half a million people continue to die each year by various strains of this disease. Dengue fever and other nasty pathogens that I was unaware of at the time are also transmitted by mosquitoes.

Many armies and military campaigns, from ancient times to the present, have come to a grinding halt due to malaria.

I didn't run out to the boonies just yet: time for vaccinations.

Under the heading of "more things that can cause death and/or distress" from the inside: cholera, tetanus, typhoid, meningitis, hepatitis, and the plague make an appearance now and again. Some of these shots are topped off every few months to maintain effectiveness.

Let's add more creepy crawly critters to the mix. Scorpions, centipedes, lizards, and spiders varied and venomous. That's right, all waiting to cozy up with you at night if you don't pay attention to where you're sleeping.

Months later, with my poncho liner covering me, almost asleep and well into the night, a family of unknown critters ran over my torso as they headed on their way. Mama critter and in single file, three or four babies. I was really in tune with my surroundings then and knew that they most likely considered me a log. I didn't even budge and returned to sleep.

Waiting in ambush, I saw them getting closer. Pesky mountain leeches, slowly inching up my boot. I'm prepared and blast them off my boot with a squirt of insect repellent. They're less of a problem once you know where to look and make sure no skin is needlessly showing for them to attach too. Should you find one (or more) on you, a bit of insect repellent or just placing your cigarette butt by them and that bloody blob will drop off (yuck). You'll be left with an itchy small mark but aside from that, you're good to go.

Between leeches, thorns, ants, and mosquitoes you won't need to be told to keep those sleeves rolled down and stay covered up. Save all those tank tops for the war movies.

Even taking these precautions, all of us seemed to have a perpetual cloud of gnats hovering around our heads. Just like Pigpen in the Charlie Brown and Snoopy cartoons, there is no getting rid of them. Morning and night I applied liberal amounts of insect repellent on my neck, face, and ankles to keep these and other critters away.

Thank God we didn't hang around in the Southern Delta regions or more rice paddies. Those swampy lowland leeches are much bigger than their mountain cousins, and believe me, you don't want them latching onto your body.

Most of the time it's just a matter of being aware of where you're sitting or standing. If not, you may soon be a candidate for the "Dancing with the Stars" TV show.

This is so true when it comes to red ants. They're everywhere, very aggressive, and if you're on their turf they'll soon convince you to move. And don't get the idea that black ants are your buddies; some have bites every bit as vicious as the red ones.

John Deere Tractors. They might as well be that, but I'm talking about water buffalo. The go-to tractor for many a local Vietnamese farm, used throughout Vietnam and Southeast Asia by farmers there. Often seen pulling a plow working in rice paddies.

Tough and hard working, many of these became casualties of war, along with the local cattle, too, intentionally and otherwise.

We had one water buffalo trip a booby trap that would've killed a few people easily, yet it continued on to disappear into the night. I felt bad for it.

Months later I hopped a chopper from Bien Hoa to visit my brother at an outlying base. The pilot had gained altitude and below us a herd of water buffalo came into view.

I saw the pilot look over to the co-pilot, nodding at the herd below and smiling. He put the chopper into a dive and skimmed over the herd, stampeding and scattering them in fear. The pilot continued the remainder of the trip hugging those tree tops, the chopper skidding just clear of the foliage below, scaring the hell out of me the whole way.

Monkeys

I rarely saw any, but they could often be heard and they could be very loud. I think they were smart enough to keep their distance, knowing the weapons we had.

Rats

Try not burying your C ration cans after a meal and you'll soon be seeing some of the biggest rats of your life. They love good GI leftovers.

Stateside

Driving along I-10 just west of Baton Rouge, Louisiana, I passed the Tiger Truck Stop many times. Not one of the big-chain truck stops, but independent. I avoided it if I could on two counts. First, it wasn't easy-on, easy-off access for my tractor trailer and parking was limited. Secondly, they kept a live tiger in a cage there as a feature draw. I'm against seeing such a magnificent animal pent up its whole life in total contradiction to its lifestyle.

Despite my reservations, one day I was tired and left no choice, so in I pulled, parked the truck, and went inside their restaurant for coffee. Sitting at a table drinking coffee, in walks a lady with two tiger cubs, one under each arm.

Now here's a sight I don't see every day, even at a tiger truck stop. I got up and strolled over to take a closer look. They were cute little cubs with paws the size of dinner plates. I hope their fate involved having more room and not spending the rest of their lives cooped up in a concrete cage.

Continue a little over a thousand miles west along the same interstate and there's a similar truck stop near Sierra Blanca, just east of El Paso, Texas. Not crazy about that place either for the same reason: the exploitation of a beautiful animal for financial gain. The cruel conditions in which they're kept and the hunting of them as trophies really upsets me.

Back to Vietnam

I never saw any tigers, though Vietnam has its share of them. I think we heard one in the mountains around Da Nang. There would be a huge roar in the distance. Very chilling.

However, we had a Recon unit that not only saw one, but killed, skinned, and brought it back to the rear. Other tigers have met similar fates with military outfits in different parts of the country. In hindsight, I'm troubled that so many of these big cats are accidentally or purposely killed in times of war.

Fido

Not many times, but on occasion we did have a military dog come out to the field with us. Highly trained to sniff out people and munitions.

Luckily they didn't hang around long enough to be involved in fire-fights, and I'm pleased to say none came to harm while with us.

Riding in a fixed-wing aircraft this time, somewhere in Vietnam, a C-123 possibly, I'm not sure. I am surrounded by a large K-9 unit. Each GI handler was teamed up with their respective German Shepard. Sitting (uneasily) close to them, I noticed how the handlers had the dog leashes loosely wrapped around the muzzle of their dogs. Nice doggie.

Bird Dog

This bird dog can fly! A mechanical kind.

OK, not a true dog, but tiny Cessna planes that "point" to the prey for the hunter like living hunting dogs. These aircraft act much the same way as pointers, targeting their prey for larger, faster aircraft, the jets.

Even at slow speed, the jets are too fast to select and pick out hidden NVA activity. Flying low and slow and every bit exposed in the way only a small Cessna can be, these courageous, maybe crazy, pilots risked their lives to pick out enemy targets. If a suitable target was found, the bird dog pilot would then fire Willie Peter (white phosphorus) rockets to mark it.

The big clouds of billowing white smoke could then be easily seen by the jets, which would come in to bomb and strafe the area.

I've seen them in action, mostly around Chu Lai. They made for a deadly one, two punch. An impressive combo.

Bao Loc

In terms of being the furthest from civilization, with some of the most rugged country I served in during my operations throughout Vietnam, Bao Loc ranked near the top. This particular mountainous area was very high in elevation; the trees became more like a pine forest than was the norm, with some open meadows with elephant grass. The nights were cool but come day, walking in that elephant grass was suffocating.

At some point we began hearing the trumpeting calls of elephants in the distance.

Wow! Real elephants. A fair-sized herd was close by. Numerous "elephant patties" started appearing on the ground. They were much larger than "cow patties" you would see down on the farm. Judging by the sound of their calls, the distance would vary.

More than once we were certain they would come into view. That led to speculation as to what to do should they charge. Still, I was really keen to see them, maybe even get a picture with my Kodak Brownie Instamatic camera.

After almost a week of dodging "elephant patties," their trumpeting calls faded to silence and our paths diverged. Maybe for the best, as I would have hated to see one come to harm.

Writing this, I'm reminded of the use of elephants by Hannibal in the Punic Wars against Rome over 2,000 years ago. Apparently there was an Asian elephant among the mostly African ones in Hannibal's army, most of which died crossing the Alps in one of the greatest military campaigns of all time.

Sadly, I understand that wild elephants in Vietnam are now almost extinct, with less than one hundred in the wild. War, poaching, loss of habitat, and the ivory trade are some of the causes for this sorry situation. When's the last time you spoke to anyone about saving Vietnamese elephants? Vietnamese elephants don't get the PR and support that you see for their larger African cousins.

I sure would've loved to see one, though, along with a (still living) tiger.

CHAPTER 22:

Cruise Ship

———◆——

THE TET OFFENSIVE THAT BROUGHT US TO SAIGON WAS
now contained and more or less under control. Our services were now
needed elsewhere, which in this case meant Da Nang.

The itinerary showed a two-day excursion up the beautiful and exotic
coastline of South Vietnam. The price of the ticket included an open bar
with beer and coke, ice and coolers not included. Good weather promised
us clear skies and calm seas.

We were traveling on a budget plan so other amenities and entertainment were kept to a minimum.

A couple of stray dogs that had found their way on board were our
entertainment and amused us with their antics. Accommodations proved
to be crowded, and berths were allocated on a first-come, first-served basis.

We were looking forward to a stress-free environment. As a bonus
feature, we were not required to pull guard duty, ensuring a full night's
sleep. Doesn't get any better than that.

Our ship was bare bones as far as cruise ships go, a far cry from the
sleek and colorful cruise ships seen plying the Caribbean Seas or sailing
north up to Alaska.

The vessel proved to be short and boxy with a paint job that did not
highlight flattery as it was built for capacity, not comfort. If you guessed

that it was a navy LST troop and vehicle transport ship, you guessed right. The crew was made up of Filipino nationals.

We were to depart from Saigon (since renamed Ho Chi Minh City, but it will always remain Saigon to me) to travel down the river to the South China Sea and then make our way north to our destination, Da Nang.

Casting off from the pier, we eased our way to deeper waters. To provide protection, Navy PT gunboats flanked each side to ward off potential ambushes. They remain with us as escorts until we hit open waters.

We reached the South China Sea without incident and made our way north. The ocean swells were not exactly the calm seas promised and some of our troops spent the trip "talking to the great white telephone."

Those of us who didn't suffer from seasickness were able to take in the sight of dolphins leaping near the bow.

Dolphins are considered lucky by cultures around the world. Their graceful presence was welcome in a business where every bit of luck was needed. Just being around them gives one a calming feeling.

What to do about the lack of ice for our drinks?

In an attempt to correct this deficiency, some of the more creative among us put the cans of coke in a sock, in one instance, and beer in a bag in another, tied a rope to the sock or bag and lowered them over the railing into the water.

This was in hopes that the water would cool the drinks down. It proved to be wishful thinking.

Hauled back up from their rough ride, the Coke cans merely do what agitated Coke cans do best, burst into a fountain of fizz. It made a better bomb than a drink.

The beer fared no better. Some smashed and—empty?

Those being the days before environmental concerns, garbage was merely tossed overboard. This buffet attracted numerous sharks. Could it be that they wanted a few beers with their meal?

It wasn't a fast ship. That was OK, slow is good. None of us were in any hurry to return to the boonies. Our itinerary was designed to create little to no stress, providing us with such activities as "not getting shot at." We weren't entirely out of the woods, though, as mines were still a concern.

A luxury feature was access to a real toilet, or "head" in navy talk, instead of the modified "outhouse" which was the norm at our base camp. That aspect alone made the cruise a luxury one.

The food remained our regular C-rations, but that's OK.

Some of us were able to sleep on the deck and catch the cool night breeze while doing some stargazing. The skies were unobstructed by the canopy of branches and total darkness of past nights.

The days did prove to be unbearably hot. If you've ever cooked with cast iron, then you know how it retains the heat once heated. The metal deck was fully exposed to the sun, and the heat retained by the all-metal construction of the vessel. Indeed, it was like sailing on a cast-iron pan.

With a lack of ventilation below it became a choice of the lessor of two evils: grilled on top or baked below.

My friend Sergeant D. of the second platoon and I were able to spend some time together and catch up on events. Though both in Charlie Company, given the way the company was often dispersed in the Boonies, we didn't cross paths much. As one of my best friends then, we shared a rare drink of Coke and shot the breeze about nothing in particular and what we'd do once we got back in "the world."

Eventually the mountainous coast of Da Nang came into view.

Just looking at those hills, my shoulders began hurting once more, thinking of the struggles we would soon be facing "humping" up those inclines. I tried to stay positive and view it as new and different territory to explore.

Later, while operating in those same mountains, high up and overlooking the South China Sea, there would be a U.S. ship firing its main guns at distant targets inland. The firing took place at night and the muzzle flash from these large guns was enormous. Many years passed and I discovered that the ship involved was Battleship New Jersey. Their 16-inch deck guns were lobbing enormous shells at NVA targets miles away.

Well, the voyage proved to be all too short. We disembarked, and there's not much I remember of Da Nang itself other than eating at a Marine Mess Hall and being allowed to return for seconds, something that was never permitted to us Stateside in the army. This was a brief respite, and before long we were back in the darkness of the triple canopy jungle.

The monsoon season was in full swing. The mist, rain, and overcast skies were all starting to wear on me.

Another unusual (for us) trip was a convoy up Highway 1. This was after we had completed our search-and-destroy operations in the Da Nang area.

With our whole brigade being moved further north to the Hue Phu Bai area, we were on our way from bad to worse. We piled into a long convoy of deuce and half-trucks and snaked our way up Highway 1. I'm not a fan of riding in any convoy. Their visibility and exposure makes too tempting a target for mines and ambushes.

Fortunately, the 60-mile trip proved uneventful, and we made it without incident—no ambushes, no mines.

CHAPTER 23:

Top Chef 2

———◆———

"Hunger is the Poor Man's sauce."

JUST AS IN THE STONE AGE WHEN SOMEONE DISCOV-
ered cooking by accidentally dropping their T-Rex steak in the fire, in a similar manner I found C-rations tasted much better when they were cooked.

Prior to going to Vietnam, the Cs I ate in the field while playing war
games for a few days at a time, were eaten cold. They didn't make a big
impression on me and I considered them rather bland.

But by cooking them, either using the "heating tabs" I've described
earlier or with C-4, that and a bit of tabasco sauce made a world of difference.

Not having access to refrigeration eliminated much of what could be
available in the Boonies.

I understand today's soldiers now eat MREs (meals ready to eat).
Never having eaten any, I can't offer an opinion as to how they compare
with Cs.

Cooking a meal involved basically the same procedure. Take out
one's stove, previously made from a C-ration can. Remove a "heating tab"
from the pantry, aka rucksack. Rip open the foil wrapping, drop it in the
"stove," and light. The soft blue flame will burn long enough to heat up one's
meal or a cup of instant coffee or hot chocolate.

A sample meal of, let's say, a canned boned chicken would be heated "as is," maybe with some tabasco sauce or salt and pepper to flavor, and away you go.

For most of us the creativity and variation came about in the cooking of different sandwiches using the canned bread.

You call this lump of barely cooked dough, bread? was my first thought when I ate it cold Stateside. However, by applying my newly discovered chef skills I was able to create some tasty sandwiches.

This was done by mixing and matching the contents of different meals/cans to create these sandwiches.

Toasted Peanut Butter and Jelly

Who doesn't like PB&J? One of my top meals. Preparation is as follows: "mis en place" as the French chefs say.

1. Have your stove and heating tab ready.

2. Take a C-ration can of bread. It's a slightly smaller can then the others.

3. Take your P-38 (can opener) and open both the top and bottom lids of the can, but not fully. The lid must remain attached to the can.

4. Remove the bread (keeping the can!). Using your chef's knife (a bayonet), cut the bread in half.

5. Then take the PB and J (they come in separate tiny cans) and spread on the bread in sandwich fashion.

6. Return the "sandwich" to the can, and bend back the lids to contain the bread. Light and drop the heating tab into the stove.

7. With your bayonet, poke a hole in the side of the can.

8. Rotate the can over the flame with the can at the end of the bayonet.

9. Slightly steamed and heated with the PB and J melted together, delicious!

10. Eat and enjoy.

The same procedure could be used to create other culinary delights such as "Toasted Ham and Cheese" sandwiches using ham slices from one can and cheese spread from another, smaller can. Variations abound, the sky's the limit.

Bear in mind that these sandwiches are about the size of an Egg McMuffin. If you have visions of a foot-long sub loaded with different toppings, you can get that out of your head. In addition, the bread cans were limited and one every meal is out of the question. Every bite was eaten slowly to savor the experience.

For dessert, our favorite: pound cake and peaches or pears.

These came in separate cans. Lids removed, the peaches would usually be eaten, leaving the juice. This would then be added to the rather dry pound cake, making a nice tasty, gooey concoction. Even fewer of these items in our Cs, so please use judiciously!

Low on the totem pole of C-rations was the Ham and Lima Bean meal. Many of our guys would discard it outright into the fire pit, such was its lack of appeal. I always kept mine. Food is food, and it's amazing what hunger does to spice up what would normally be considered unappetizing.

Moving on to what are considered some of the "Primo" meals in our pantry, these were known as LRRPs. The name came about due to the fact that these meals were initially given to Long Range Reconnaissance Patrols.

We got these off and on and they were a treat. Don't count on having some every resupply.

These were freeze dried, self-contained meals (like Spaghetti and Meatballs) and came in individual vacuum packs. Cutting edge for that period, similar meals are common these days and found in any sporting goods stores such as Cabela's or Pro Bass Shop.

Using a heating "tab" and water heated in one's canteen cup, merely cut open the top of the LRRP of your choice, pour in the water, and stir. The LRRP pack itself acts as the container.

Yum, like you died and went to heaven.

Rice? No, we weren't issued any, but the Vietnamese interpreters and interrogators who traveled with our company would carry rations that better suited their diet. They would contain rice, dried fish, and various spices. I love rice but never ate any in the field.

Some of our troops would barter for the rice. I later found out that it was a good deal if for no other reason than the fact that rice bulks up to twice its size when cooked. This makes a little go a long way when it comes to weight calculations.

However, early in my Tour, I did trade for some of their dried fish (my objective there was to lighten my rucksack). Very salty and tasting a lot like anchovies, but without the pizza.

I soon gave up on that idea and went back to the Cs.

More to come…

CHAPTER 24:

Top Chef 1

———◆—◆———

TOP CHEF—LET'S TALK CHOW, A LONG OVERDUE TOPIC.
I'm not sure if I can complete this in one sitting.

Less than five miles from where I live is Schoolcraft College. Its culinary school ranks as one of the top three culinary schools in the United States and has produced two winners in the TV cooking reality show "Top Chef."

I have taken some of their Continuing Education Classes in cooking and I can vouch for their excellent curriculum. Love these classes. Your main task as a student is to eat the meals the Chef and his students prepare. Twist my arm.

Schoolcraft also has an excellent restaurant and bakery that is run by the culinary staff and students. They've recently added a new wing that contains a brewery and have begun offering beer-brewing classes along with wine-making courses already offered. Yes, my name is on the list for an upcoming beer-brewing class.

I have benefited from their excellent online writing classes (ED2GO), the byproduct of which has given me the confidence to tackle this book. They also have excellent math classes (yes, I've taken a couple) and the students rank at the top of the list for math students across the United States.

One of my favorite senior chefs there is also a Vietnam Vet (Navy). I think I'll be getting his input and perspective on this topic before all is said and done.

C-Rations: The Basics

C-Rations were by far our main food source and comprised the bulk of our meals. Before setting out to the Boonies, we would be supplied with a complete case of C-rations, containing 12 individual meals in separate boxes.

The word "ration" in "C-ration" had a dual meaning. It's our food, so we had to make sure not to overeat and take from future meals, as that case had to last to the next resupply day four days away.

Math alert: 4 x 3 = 12. Start pigging out and eating two meals in a sitting will see you run out of food before the next resupply. You learn early to eat sparingly and with moderation.

Same goes for our water. You have what you can carry; nobody is going to carry anything for you. Sip, don't guzzle. Over-drink and run out? Tough s**t. Forget even asking anyone for a bit of theirs. On average, we would carry a minimum of four canteens, but carry as much as you want. It all comes down to what your pain quotient is.

Which goes to say we are always on the edge of hunger and thirst. We'd love seconds or thirds, given the amount of calories we burn.

Speaking of calories, these were the days before the nutrition listings were marked on cans, so sodium, sugar, fat, etc.—couldn't tell you.

Here is an overview of the contents of the main meals.

Boned turkey. Ham and eggs. Chopped spiced beef. Beef slices and potatoes. Turkey loaf. Beefsteak. Ham and lima beans. Porky steak. Boned chicken. Fried ham. Chicken and noodles.

Coffee, tea, hot chocolate.

These meals in turn contained dessert cans that could be pears, peaches, pound cake, chocolate. Smaller tins of bread, peanut butter, jelly, and cheese and crackers were also included. A tin of bread was critical. Hated that canned bread Stateside. In 'Nam with my newfound chef skills, however, it became a favorite.

Supplementary meals, LRRP's, rice, sundries. More on that later.

Can openers. No electric outlets for your electric can opener. The hand-crank type seen on many kitchen counters was too bulky. No, we had the trusty, ever reliable P-38, known far and wide to all GIs there. A small thumbnail-size metal can opener well-suited for the job, which was tiny and light for storage.

One of our canteen pouches held a canteen cup. Metal with a foldout handle, it served as a pot to heat whatever but mostly coffee, hot chocolate, and tea.

Many of us received instant Kool Aid in the mail from home. We often added it to the water in our canteens to make some of our water better tasting.

All water in any event required halazone (chlorine-based) tablets to purify the water.

Drop in one per canteen and wait five minutes for it to do its purification thing. Most of our water was from surrounding streams and rivers.

To heat our meals: wood stove? Nope. They went by the name of "heating tabs." They came in a heavy foil pack, similar in size to Alka-Seltzer tablets. We would grab as many as were needed. They burned with a blue, smokeless flame and suited the job. A single tab was sufficient to heat one's coffee or meal. To light it up, my Zippo, of course (I was a heavy smoker in those days). The stove would be constructed from one of the used C-ration cans. Take a "church key" and punch holes around the top and bottom edges of the can for ventilation, and instant stove. Drop the heating tab inside and light it, and then set your canteen cup on top of the can to be heated. This homemade stove could be used multiple times.

We had a CE (combat engineer) in our platoon who had ample supplies of C-4, which was a deadly explosive detonated by means of a blasting cap. Yet when lit with a match, it did not present a problem and it burned like a charm with an intense heat.

I never used it, but I understand it was a good alternative to the heating tabs. Pricey though, considered what it was really intended for.

Cutlery

Disposable spoons were included with the C-rations, so we didn't keep using the same one over and over. Hepatitis C, dysentery, and all manner of nasty things could result from that. Our fine china is the cans themselves. Use once, dig a hole, and bury the empties. If you don't bury them, all manner of real "Boonie rats" will be attracted. Plus any number of ants and other pests.

Also, we want to leave as little sign of our presence as possible in the Boonies.

CHAPTER 25:

Unpleasant Odors

———◆—◆———

Montreal, P.Q.

IT REMAINS ONE OF MY EARLIEST MEMORIES. I WAS VERY young, and as it was connected to the sense of smell, just the odd whiff of the offending odor is enough to bring the whole event back.

I remember being wheeled into the operating room, fully trusting the doctor and nurses.

I was about to go under the knife to get either my tonsils out or circumcision, one or both—they must of had a two-for-one deal going.

The anesthesiologist said to me, "Relax kid, this won't hurt a bit" or words to that effect. I did, and he put the mask on me.

The overwhelming smell of the ether had an immediate negative effect on me. What I was told only took 10 to 15 seconds before losing consciousness seemed like a half an hour. I was all legs and arms trying to get away, and had to be held down.

I woke up with the operation a success. Liberal servings of ice cream aided my recovery.

However, I never recovered from my suspicions of the medical establishment or the memory of the smell of ether.

Ether is no longer used as an anesthetic today. But it still appears in a number of other products, such as starter aerosol spray for diesel engines. A few molecules of ether hitting my nose and that's all I can take. It all comes back.

Somewhere Near Hue, Phu Bai, Way Out in the Boonies

It used to be that perfume ads in magazines would have "scratch and sniff" tabs to advertise their products. The accompanied pictures of nicely designed perfume bottles packaged with the sense of smell—all designed to entice the customer to make a purchase.

If the scene I'm about to describe was packaged in "scratch and sniff" ads and placed on recruiting posters, many would reconsider their choices.

Another Kind of Smell

(Alert: The following is disturbing.)

Making our way through the Boonies west of Hue.

As we move up the trail, an intense buzzing noise increases along with the smell associated with it. It sounds much like a hive of bees swarming. I had an inkling of what was coming.

The tight, narrow trail took a sharp bend to my right and I adjusted my footing just in time.

I was already covering my mouth with my towel and trying not to breathe or gag before viewing the inevitable.

Laying on his back, face up, what was left of it. Dead about a week. Head, skull, half blown away on the vertical axis. Body, bloated and blackened with his uniform stretched skin tight. A mass of flies hovered with the noise of a beehive. Looking down, while trying not to look at the same time, I see the part of his body I almost tripped over.

A solid mass of writhing white maggots from his knee to his boot. Too late to avert my gaze.

The whole mess is partially submerged in a puddle of muddy water. The heat and humidity frame the sickening scene with greater intensity. In a slight opening, up the trail a bit, more dead NVA bodies, equally sickening to see. Some clumped in foxholes indistinguishable from the next. They were the result of a firefight a week before in an encounter with one of our units.

Some of our of guys half-heartedly toss our calling cards on the corpses. Ace of Spades or the "Widow Maker, O'Deuce" ones.

Later that day, the company splits as we prepare to go on patrol. The CO wanted our squad to return past that disgusting mess and set up an ambush. Was he kidding? To what end? "F**k you, mother-f**ker!" was our thought in response.

After much protesting it was agreed that we should only go up to a point where the smell wasn't too bad to place our ambush.

Thanks a lot.

That evening I unlaced my boots to change socks and discover the putrid smell from the NVA body had soaked into my boots. A perfume of death I could well do without. It lingered on me for the better part of the week.

I wrote the following poem shortly after that day. The title is because what I saw could well be me…should I be that unlucky.

Death's Mirror
A maggot's meal, their stench unreal,
The bodies lie in open sky.
That horrid gaze, which leaves you dazed,
An image formed that can't be torn.
And sears into ongoing thought, the fear, the dread,
Of the next onslaught.

Note: Unlike in populated areas, where the dead are disposed of for obvious reasons, in the Boonies they were left to rot in place.

CHAPTER 26:

Resupply

———➤◆◄———

POW! POP!

(I'm working on my sound effects.)

Followed by a shower of hot peanut butter, maybe molten jelly, sometimes cheese.

To experience a more realistic effect, throw a small can of, let's say, beans in your next campfire and listen for the sound yourself.

What's going on? Are we being shelled by the NVA with a new type of food artillery?

No, our fire pit is burning the trash, cartons, discarded and torn clothing, miscellaneous items, C-ration boxes, and whatever. A rough hole had been dug and the fire would be burning for a while. The final process of cleaning up our resupply LZ. In every resupply we are given a full case of C-rations containing 12 meals, each with an assortment of canned food, the above three being a sample.

If you had an older-style M16 with the open three-prong flash suppressor, you could use it to insert into the baling wire that's securing the case of Cs. With a quick twist of the '16, the wire would snap, allowing you to remove the C-ration cans to dig into your rations. Cans and rations would be removed and packed into the rucksack to minimize space used. Gone is the big, square, space-inefficient box.

The carton case would go into the fire pit along with the cardboard boxes of the individual meals and needless duplicates of items like spoons, paper, and so on.

And yes, certain unopened cans of food considered less desirable by some of us would also find their way there. No one had an issue with tossing unwanted cans of food into the fire. The problem comes from not putting a hole in the cans first.

The cans, heated by the fire, expand, swell, and eventually explode with a noise much louder than you think their size would permit. The contents come raining down indiscriminately on everybody. Hey, you get your humor where you can.

General cussin' and jokes about the anonymous culprits are voiced.

Threats are made about military discipline being inflicted if it happens one more time (but it always happens one more time).

The only ones not laughing too hard are those with molten jelly running down their face, or gobs of peanut butter stuck to their helmet.

We're not too concerned about noise discipline during this whole time. The greater noise of choppers coming and going most of the day and the fire leaves no mystery as to our presence. Once on the move we'll go back to making ourselves invisible.

So what is this resupply thing?

The term is pretty self-explanatory. We'll be out here in the Boonies for a few weeks. Come the end of four days, our C-rations are mostly consumed and it's time to stock up. A landing zone (LZ) will be selected and resupply choppers will be radioed to drop off what we requested.

This will be repeated every four days until the operation ends.

Water we acquire as need be in the course of our day-to-day patrols while moving through the bush, normally from a mountain stream. Fill up our four canteens or so, pop in the halazon purification pill, wait five minutes (and you had best wait five minutes! It doesn't matter how thirsty you are), and you're good to go. If you don't wait, you risk getting any number of nasty things growing inside of you.

Aside from the anticipation of getting our Cs replenished, resupply is welcomed from the standpoint of having that much less of the day devoted to patrols and the stress that goes with them. An added bonus is getting to see some of our buddies in other platoons as the company gathers together. I look upon it as the weekend in our four-day workweek.

First things first: We have to select and prep the intended resupply area. This is often a hilltop without a ton of vegetation that needs clearing. Ideally the choppers want to swoop in, hover at about three to four feet, chuck those Cs out the door, and be on their way.

Though we might have picked a fairly secure LZ, all those choppers coming and going make for targets on a sniper's shooting range.

OK, we found a spot. Machetes come out, and the clearing begins. I wish I could say we had chainsaws for the larger trees.

For some of the stubborn ones, did I mention we have C4? Better than anything you can find at your local Home Depot. A bit of strategically applied "fire in the hole" and problem solved.

Done. The choppers are radioed and given the go-ahead to come on down.

A Trooper pops yellow smoke, and it billows out, identifying the LZ. The same Trooper positions himself in front of the approaching chopper, arms upraised, guiding him in. It slows, and flares to a stop hovering there, with the crew chief leaning out inspecting the LZ.

Elephant grass is waving crazily, and branches, yellow smoke, grass, and twigs fly into the air as it's all sucked up by the rotor wash. The crew chief radios telling us the area needs more clearing and is unsafe as it is. The chopper books out.

SOB. Out come the machetes and there's more sweating, chopping, hacking, and cursing. Threats against the crew chief's well-being are made.

Finally all looks good, done.

Again the lead chopper is called in, and this time the LZ is given a thumbs up.

One after another in quick succession come a string of choppers. Cs are tossed out, a Chaplin maybe disembarks on one, or maybe some visiting Brass, and possibly replacement troops. Ammo is topped off or replaced.

It's a routine we've done many times, and the parade of choppers do their thing without any wasted motion.

They approach, flare, hover, out fly the Cs, the chopper picks up revs, banks down the sides of the mountain, and in a graceful swoop, is gone, the slap of the rotors fading as he picks up altitude in the distance.

CHAPTER 27:

Tools of Death...and Beyond

———◆———

WHO KNEW THAT I LIVED IN THE HEART OF THE MILI-
tary-industrial complex, near the manufacturer of one of the greatest
weapons of all time.

The AK-47? The M16?

Nope. I'm talking about the Daisy BB Gun, once manufactured right
here in Plymouth, Michigan.

Oh how I wanted one as a kid, and was consistently denied my
dream by my mom. My repeated requests always met with the universal
answer given by mothers everywhere. You'll probably end up shooting
your brother in the eye, or vice versa.

It's a measure of the effectiveness of today's standard infantry weapons that they remain basically unchanged for over fifty years. Believe me,
if the military could find a better infantry weapon that could kill, maim,
and mutilate people in as short a time as possible, and as cost effectively,
we would have it by now.

They are the M16 for the U.S. Army and the AK-47 used by many
opposing forces throughout the world. During my time in Vietnam,
the transition had largely taken place from the heavier and longer M14
(both the rifle itself and the ammo it used) to the much lighter M16
and its correspondingly lighter ammo. Both are capable of firing on full
or semiautomatic.

The ongoing debate continues, which is better? Depends on who you talk to; there are pros and cons for both.

The AK-47, the slightly heavier weapon with heavier ammo, comes with a 30-round clip. It also comes with a larger-caliber round (7.62) than the M16, with its .223 caliber round. At the time I was in the Army, we had a 20-round clip for the M16. That's now been bumped up to a 30-round clip. The AK-47 is known to be able to take a lot of abuse and dirt, which is a key feature making it a favorite to many.

What the M16 lacks in its smaller round is made up for with its extremely high velocity, causing great internal damage to whoever is unfortunate enough to be at the receiving end.

A big drawback is its high susceptibility to dirt, grit, and dust. In addition to regular cleaning and lubrication, extra care and awareness are needed to make sure it stays dirt free.

The NVA had the RPD as their machine gun. Its ammo came in a circular canister of about 100 rounds. An advantage of having ammo in a canister is that it's protected from dirt. The NVA also had RPGs (rocket-propelled grenades), a mean weapon.

Tracer ammo was used in most of our weapons, not including the M79. For the M60, every fifth round was a tracer. For the M16, I would load every other round as a tracer. Tracers could be colored green or red. Ours were always red.

Anything larger than the M60, the .50 caliber for us or the .51 caliber for the NVA, is classed as a heavy machine gun. Heavier in caliber and weight, they're not something you're just going to be throwing over your shoulder and heading down the trail with. At over 80 pounds without ammo or a tripod base, they were best left at firebases or rear-area bunkers.

The majority of firefights I've been in were in very close quarters, and having tracer rounds to instantly adjust my aim was a big help.

For the machine gun we carried the M60. It was fed ammo that came in 100-round links. These could be further clipped together in firefights to keep the gun fed so it could fire in a continuous fashion. The machine gunner had an assistant gunner whose job it was to link these belts as needed, keeping them out of the dirt, while reminding the gunner to fire in "bursts" so as to not overheat the barrel.

A problem with the ammo links was their exposure to constant moisture and debris collecting from bushes, trees, and dirt. All these factors added up, and if the rounds were not used before they get too funky, well, the '60 had a very good chance of jamming.

In firefights, the barrel could and would get very hot. I'm talking red hot. However, it came with an interchangeable barrel as a backup (oh joy, more weight for the '60 gunner to carry). It had a spotty reputation for jamming and was not popular in some circles. My platoon sergeant (on his second tour) was not a fan, and would not allow anyone under his command to carry a '60.

When it did work correctly, which was most of the time in the firefights I was involved in, it was very effective in laying down that lead.

Grenades (frag or Willie Peter), help yourself to as many as you want. Claymore mines, technically a weapon since they're normally triggered by hand, same thing. We had LAWS (light antitank weapons), sort of a one-shot disposable bazooka that replaced the 3.5 rocket launcher. Ideal for busting bunkers.

The 1911 .45 Colt was the standard pistol issued then, which some of us were authorized to carry. It is no longer issued as newer makes and models have been introduced. The 9-mm replacement has itself now been replaced.

Our platoon came out from a tree line to the edge of big expanse of rice paddies. Across and in the far distance and looking very tiny (I remember guessing about 600 yards), was a lone Vietnamese. Beyond the effective range of our M16s but not the '60. The Vietnamese was out in the open on the opposite edge of the rice paddies from us.

The '60 gunner was quickly ordered to the forefront to fire away and take down the Vietnamese. The gunner scrambled to extend the legs of the bipod stabilizing the '60. Then he got in the prone position, aimed, and fired. The gun jammed! But not before it got one round off.

I was standing a bit behind the gunner watching the round (a tracer) describe a seemingly slow red arc as it traveled to its intended target.

The Vietnamese didn't sense the danger that "arc of death" posed as it traced its way to him. The round seemed to catch him in the thigh region.

He dropped. Too far away to hear any screams, if indeed, he did.

Our gunner was frantically trying to get his '60 working, while out of the tree line in the vicinity of the hit Vietnamese, a half dozen tiny figures appeared, running to rescue their fallen comrade. The distance between us made their dash appear very slow. Yet they did manage to drag him to cover.

The gun remained jammed. We opened up with M16s, which didn't seem to find their mark, and the targets faded into the tree line, dragging their fallen comrade in tow.

Grenades: More Detail

The most common were the HE (high explosive), and we would carry easily upwards of a dozen. They had a smooth outer casing. Inside a coil of wire surrounded the C4 explosive and a blasting cap ran through the middle, attached to the pin/firing pin/pull ring. Pull the safety pin, and once you let the firing handle go, detonation would follow, after a count of approximately 4 seconds.

Smoke Grenades

The two most common were yellow and red smoke. Cylindrical in shape and bigger than the HE, they would billow out dense clouds of smoke when activated.

Yellow was used to mark and direct resupply choppers to a landing. Red was used to direct and mark enemy targets, most commonly for gunships (armed helicopters) or other aircraft.

CS gas was a stronger military version of tear gas, and we had a few around that would be used in tunnels.

Willie Peter was a real nasty device and woe to you should you pick up any shrapnel from this baby. Larger and more cylindrical than a regular HE frag, the shrapnel itself was mostly white phosphorus, which because of its chemical nature, continues to burn until exhausted. I carried only one. I kept it in reserve as a last resort if I thought we were in danger of being overrun. I had no intention of ever letting myself be captured.

Flamethrowers were your own portable (but heavy!) napalm kit. I never saw one in action, though they were used and were ideal for knocking out enemy bunkers. That is, as long as an NVA tracer didn't put a round in your tank first!

We did have "specialty" units and commandos that were trained on long-range sniper rifles. Some of our LRRPs (long-range reconnaissance patrols) were allowed their weapon of choice. Some would choose AKs, and even the odd Thompson Machine Gun.

Bayonets: Everyone had one.

Assorted hunting knifes: It was left up to the individual. We just had to remember that all that extra weight adds up fast.

Night-vision goggles: Very primitive at the time. I recall a large, not exactly portable, version we had at a rear-area bunker. Bulky and still in the prototype stage then, they had quite a ways to go before they would shrink to the size of what is available these days.

GPS: Oh, do I wish. Your basic map and compass, a good skill to know just the same. Batteries not required.

Most of the weapons above fall under the classification of "small arms," a misnomer if ever there was one.

The Bigger, Badder Weapons

Heavier-caliber weapons: .50-caliber machine gun, 81-m or 4.2 mortars. Too heavy or large to tote in the field, as a rule they augmented the defense perimeter of firebases.

Anti-aircraft guns, SAMs (surface to air missiles)

Quad .50s, 20-mm canons with explosive tips, rockets in all their different configurations, napalm, bombs (250, 500, 1000, 2000 pounds), numerous types of rockets. Cluster bombs, mines, Agent Orange, the list went on.

Mike Perry, squatting and holding an AK47,Bob
Britt standing behind him .

RTO Prescott, face bandaged from a wound.
Lt Thomas, looking back over his shoulder,

Above
Firefight in progress.

Capt. Anderson , (pointing)

Forward Observer (FO), Silva, (maps in pocket),
calling in a Fire Mission (Artillery)

Below

Me.-- Pete (Pierre) Major at Ft Campbell,Ky - dedicating
a memorial to the fallen of the O'Deuce (2/502)
-our battalion in the 101st Airborne Division.

Above

Change of Command in the Field.

Capt. Godboldte (on left) outgoing - to - the new C.O.
Capt. Anderson, on the far right.
I served under them both.

Above

Firefight
Trooper on his right in the midst of tossing a Frag (grenade).
M 60 gunner on left laying down covering fire (can
see shell casing flying out to the right).

Above

From left; Dan Perry, Mike Perry, Bob Britt, Myself

On our way to the O'Deuce (101st) Reunion, paying respects at Capt. Anderson's grave.

Above
Firefight in Progress

Sgt. Mike Perry (standing) marking an enemy
position for the Machine Gun (the 60).

My motorcycle in the foreground, taking a break at Rice Lake,Wi.
On our way to the 2/502, 1st Bde. , 101st Reunion in Chicago.

Mike Perry (lf), Bob Britt (rt)

At Ft Campbell, Ky. At the dedication of the our
Battalion Memorial for those killed in Vietnam.

Me ??

A number of people in my Platoon claim this is me, I'm not entirely sure.

I was right! I've been told his name is Duke.

Firefight in progress

Above

Al Zbik (lf), Art Goldsmith, (rt)

On the Chicago Water Taxi, taking in the sights
at the O'Deuce reunion.,2018

Below
Picture, courtesy of Al Zbik, holding his M 79, towel
around neck. Prescott in the background

Sgt Britt by downed Resupply Chopper

Below
3rd Platoon, (aka, Fletcher's Fighters),Co. C ,
2/502, 1st Bde., 101st Airborne division

Sgt Fletcher on the far left, Lt. Thomas on the far right.

Me, back row, near the center (with glasses), we
had just come back from the barber shop

Taken at our ,then, Base Camp in Phan Rang,
Nov 1967 during a Stand Down.
It was back to the Boonies the next day.

Below
Squad picture, Taken in the boonies.

Back row, from left, Frank Aragon, Pete Major (me,
holding my M 79), Sgt. Chagois,,on right-??

Front row, from left, unknown , Al Painter, Reynolds
I have Frank to thank for this picture, as it was taken with his camera and one of the very few pictures I have of myself in Vietnam.

Below

Al Painter ,left (one of my best friends) ,wound on his hand received in a firefight on my final day in the Boonies. Unfortunately he died in an auto accident in the 90's before I had a chance to meet him once more. We all missed his Wacky sense of humor.

Art Goldsmith on the right. Attended his first reunion recently in Chicago after more than 50 years without seeing any of us. After Vietnam he went on to continue his career in the Army, some of it in Special Forces. Served with distinction and is highly decorated. Still decorations do little to compensate for the PTSD he has to cope with.

Albert "Zeke" Zbik, a fellow Trooper in my Platoon
Al Zbik's Shadow Box – Line#1,Jump Wings 2/ CIB 3/ small
round button, widow maker logo pin (not official military issue)
4/Glider Patch 5/ 101st Screaming Eagle shoulder patch 6/
18th Medical Brigade Shoulder patch 7/Class A US brass, 8/
Purple Heart award. Small rectangle Good conduct award
Top row: Ribbon: purple heart, good conduct
Bottom row: National defense ribbon, Vietnam ser-
vice award with 2 battle stars.
Vietnam campaign medal
Army sharpshooter badge for pistol and rifle

Good Conduct Medal(red)
Vietnam Service Medal with 2 battle stars
St. Christopher Medal (patron saint of travels)
Jewish Mezuzah
Jewish Star of David
Military issue Dog tags , Name tag class A Uniform,
101st Airborne Commemorative coin

I haven't done it yet, but I'm starting to construct my own Shadow Box

Top: CIB , Combat Infantryman's Badge

My Jump wings (made into a bracelet)

On the right , 101st Division Patch, 82nd Division Patch(bottom)

Bottom left, Battalion Insignia, 2/502

DISTINGUISHED
SERVICE CROSS

HEADQUARTERS, UNITED STATES ARMY VIETNAM

APO SAN FRANCISCO 93675

GENERAL ORDERS NUMBER 836, 23 FEBRUARY 1968

BY DIRECTION OF THE PRESIDENT, THE DISTINGUISHED SERVICE CROSS IS
AWARDED TO SERGEANT MICHAEL P. PERRY,   UNITED STATES
ARMY, COMPANY C, 2ND BATTALION, 502ND INFANTRY, 1ST BRIGADE, 101ST
AIRBORNE DIVISION FOR EXTRAORDINARY HEROISM IN CONNECTION WITH MILITARY
OPERATIONS INVOLVING CONFLICT WITH AN ARMED HOSTILE FORCE IN THE
REPUBLIC OF VIETNAM. SERGEANT PERRY (THEN SPECIALIST FOUR) DISTINGUISHED
HIMSELF BY EXCEPTIONALLY VALOROUS ACTIONS ON 29 SEPTEMBER 1967 WHILE
SERVING AS SQUAD LEADER OF AN AIRBORNE INFANTRY COMPANY ON A SEARCH
AND DESTROY MISSION NEAR CHU LAI. THE FORWARD PLATOONS OF THE COMPANY
RECEIVED A HEAVY VOLUME OF ENEMY AUTOMATIC WEAPONS FIRE THAT PINNED
THEM DOWN AND INFLICTED SEVERAL CASUALTIES. SERGEANT PERRY'S PLATOON
WAS CONTACTED AND REQUESTED TO MOVE FORWARD AND FLANK THE VIET CONG.
WHILE ADVANCING TOWARD ITS SISTER ELEMENTS, HIS UNIT WAS SUDDENLY
SUBJECTED TO INTENSE HOSTILE FIRE FROM FORTIFIED AND WELL CONCEALED
BUNKERS. WHILE THE REST OF THE TROOPS PROVIDED SUPPORTING FIRE,
SERGEANT PERRY AND HIS PLATOON SERGEANT CHARGED THROUGH A HAIL OF
BULLETS, FIRING THEIR RIFLES AND THROWING HAND GRENADES INTO THE
VIET CONG POSITIONS. SEVERAL ENEMY GRENADES LANDED NEAR SERGEANT
PERRY, AND HE UNHESITANTLY GRABBED THEM AND HURLED THEM BACK AT
THE INSURGENTS. ALTHOUGH WOUNDED BY FRAGMENTS FROM AN EXPLODING
GRENADE, HE REFUSED TO WITHDRAW FOR MEDICAL TREATMENT AND CONTINUED
HIS FIERCE ASSAULT UNTIL HE HAD DESTROYED FOUR ENEMY BUNKERS. HE
THEN QUICKLY HELPED REORGANIZE THE PLATOON'S TROOPS AND LED THEM
TO RELIEVE THEIR BELEAGUERED COMRADES. WHEN SAVAGE AUTOMATIC WEAPONS
FIRE AGAIN ERUPTED ON THE PLATOON, SERGEANT PERRY AND HIS PLATOON
SERGEANT BRAVED MURDEROUS FIRE TO ASSAULT A VIET CONG POSITION,
SUCCESSFULLY DESTROYING IT WITH HAND GRENADES. HAVING EXPENDED
HIS GRENADES, SERGEANT PERRY ARMED HIMSELF WITH ENEMY GRENADES AND
CONTINUED HIS ATTACK THROUGH A CURTAIN OF FIRE. WITH BULLETS STRIKING
ALL AROUND THEM, SERGEANT PERRY AND HIS COMRADE GALLANTLY ASSAULTED
AND DESTROYED BUNKER AFTER BUNKER. THE REMAINING INSURGENTS WERE
FORCED TO FLEE THE BATTLEFIELD. HIS FEARLESS AND DETERMINED ACTIONS
IN CLOSE COMBAT RESULTED IN THE ELIMINATION OF NINE ENEMY BUNKERS,
EIGHTEEN VIET CONG KILLED AND NUMEROUS WEAPONS CAPTURED. SERGEANT
PERRY'S EXTRAORDINARY HEROISM AND DEVOTING TO DUTY WERE IN KEEPING
WITH THE HIGHEST TRADITIONS OF THE MILITARY SERVICE AND REFLECT
GREAT CREDIT UPON HIMSELF, HIS UNIT, AND THE UNITED STATES ARMY.

Above is a copy of Mike Perry's orders awarding him the Distinguished
Service Cross for Valor, the nation's second highest award for Valor.

The Actions depicted above took place at
the same time I arrived in Vietnam.

We both served in the 3rd Platoon Co C, 2/502 at roughly the
same time and at one point he was my Squad leader.

Pierre (Pete) Major

He was a great Trooper to serve with and goes without
saying a definite asset to our Company.

Mike was able to track me down in the early 90's which led to Reunions
with many of my fellow Troopers. Prior to that I had zero contact
with anyone from my Company and ceased to think I ever would.
It also led to me connecting with the VA sys-
tem and getting help with some of my issues.

CHAPTER 28:

Two Garbage Dumps

---◆---

IT WAS IN THE REAR AREA IN BIEN HOA. I WAS TAPPED for a work detail which involved riding in the back of a Deuce half-truck hauling garbage to the our local military garbage dump.

Similar to garbage dumps everywhere. Food waste, cardboard, scraps of whatever, smelly.

Three of us rode in the back of the truck, picking a spot to stand among the trash. The other GI with me was also picked at random from another unit and unknown to me.

We weren't along to empty the truck; we would soon have plenty of help in that department. That help was to come from the groups of orphans living in the dump. Days before, in his enthusiasm to climb on the truck for the choice pickings, a kid was caught up in the wheel well and died.

Our mission was to prevent the kids from scampering up onto the truck before it came to a full stop. After which they'd be free to empty the contents and help themselves to the trash.

Approaching the garbage mound, many kids ranging in age from just past toddlers to early teens were gathering and making their way in our direction. To the whole unpleasant sight was added the unpleasant smell of what you would expect from a garbage dump in humid, 100+ degree heat.

Just before reaching the dump, me and my fellow GI already had our hands full shoeing and trying to ward off some of the more aggressive older kids. A few I had to pick up by the hand and drop away from the truck to keep order.

Finally, safely, we came to a stop. The orphans piled on, grabbing for the choicest scraps. It looked like a mad medley for a while; still, I could see that a definite pecking order existed in the chaos. The older, stronger kids invited themselves and their helpers to the best pickings. They knew what they were after and got to it first.

In no time flat they had mostly emptied the truck and little remained. It was about then that one kid threw something at the GI working with me and it caught him in the head.

He immediately went berserk and started swinging at any kid within reach. The kids went flying. Some from the force of his blows, the rest to avoid them. It was all over in five seconds. I managed to get the GI quieted down.

One little kid, not more than maybe five, wasn't so lucky. He sat on the pile of garbage, bleeding from the face and crying, a victim of those blows.

It wasn't a shining moment in my life reflecting I did nothing to help or console the kid.

The events play back in my mind now and again, watching the poor kid crying as our truck slowly pulled away to return to base.

One more sad tragic story of the many experienced and brought about by the circumstances of war.

Months Earlier

Way out in the Boonies, our resupply had been completed earlier in the day. We could see some of the black smoke that hung over the hill we had recently occupied, growing more distant as the day progressed. Smoke from fires we lit to burn anything the enemy might find useful.

We were already well along in making slow progress up an opposing hillside.

This area had a heavy VC/NVA presence, and having one of our guys killed a few days past added to our gloomy feeling. Adding to our aggravation was a sniper taking pot shots at us.

Here and there, the smoke and view of our receding resupply site would become visible through breaks in the foliage.

Then little figures of what were women and kids picking through the leftovers of our dump became apparent.

I wasn't surprised about what was to take place.

Growing in sound as they approached, first visible as little puffs of smoke dotting the sky just above the resupply site. Finally the burst of the exploding shells make it to our ears.

Artillery air bursts had them scattering for cover.

Not the one to call in this fire mission, I was nevertheless complicit in my anger to see it come about. Anger brought about from the thought that they could so easily profit from our supplies, trash or no trash.

Killing from a distance, easier than up close. Killing in any event.

Troubling too was that fact that I didn't lose any sleep over the events of that day.

Was I evolving into a "not very nice person?"

Not pleasant to think about, not pleasant to recall.

CHAPTER 29:
December 1967

DECEMBER 1967 PROVED TO BE A CRITICAL AND PIVOTAL month for me in at least three ways.

1. An incident that happened to me on the day after Christmas. It was one of those things that one can tie to a particular point in time and that puts a mark on the calendar for the remainder of one's life. It requires a bit of telling, so I'll reserve it for a stand-alone narrative. In fact, it was this one story that initiated this series of narratives. It took place on Christmas Day 1967.

2. The remainder of the 101st Airborne Division arrived from the United States to join us (First Brigade, 101st Airborne) and established the rear area for the 101st at Bien Hoa, which is near Saigon.

   For the majority of the time prior to their arrival, the rear area of the 101st was maintained at Phan Rang. In my mind it was a more picturesque, safe, and desirable, (on the coast of the South China Sea) place than Bien Hoa.

3. One of my brothers, Brian, also arrived in Vietnam along with the remaining contingent of the 101st. He was attached to the Third Brigade, and served most of his tour as a Radio Operator

in Phan Thiet. How he got that MOS when it was denied me I've yet to figure out.

While in Vietnam, I was not aware that Brian was in the army, let alone the 101st.

His presence was made known to me by administration in our battalion. I was further given the option of being assigned out of Infantry and to a safer rear area duty.

I declined, having bonded with my outfit. At the time I was determined to see my one-year tour through. Still, I kept that option in my back pocket.

Two years younger than me, our teenage years were difficult and made more so by my parents' divorce at the time. Given today's hindsight, but unknown to me at the time, was the manifestation of schizophrenia that was making itself felt in his life then.

Schizophrenia is a serious mental illness that interferes with a person's ability to think clearly, manage emotions, make decisions, and relate to others. It is a complex, long-term medical illness, affecting about 1% of Americans—that's over three million Americans!

– From the National Alliance of Mental Illness (NAMI) website (https://www.nami.org/).

I urge anyone to check it out for insights into this very difficult/complex illness.

I knew something wasn't right going back to our teenage years but couldn't put my finger on it and it wasn't until he left Vietnam that a full-blown psychotic episode resulted in a proper diagnosis. This took place during his final year in the Army while stationed back Stateside.

The illness progressed over the years to the point where he became 100% disabled. His struggles with Schizophrenia occupied most of his adult life. His life ended earlier this year in large part due to complications resulting from his illness.

There is no cure for schizophrenia, but it can be managed with drugs that are somewhat better than what was available at that time.

When I spoke to him about his time in Vietnam he says his time there wasn't all that bad.

He wasn't in the Infantry, and much of his time was spent on a mountaintop communication outpost. Contrasted with my day-to-day humping the Boonies, I considered it relatively safe.

I say "relatively" safe.

At one point they were rocketed daily for almost two weeks straight, with his bunker narrowly avoiding being hit. Not without their perils.

In any event I had no contact with Brian throughout my tour in Vietnam until just before I left the place and I had an opportunity to visit him. He had a pretty good set up at the time. However, I wasn't pleased with the amount of drugs he was doing. I let him know as much but without effect.

I'm happy to say that he made it through his tour in Vietnam without incident.

His real troubles were yet to begin with a psychotic breakdown during his final year in the Army.

I believe the hallucinogenic drugs he was taking at the time, combined with his schizophrenia were the main factors in his breakdown.

CHAPTER 30:

Sappers

———————◆◆◆———————

SONG BE. LESS THAN 10 "CLICKS" FROM THE CAMBODIAN
border.

It was the beginning of another nameless operation in the Boonies.
In typical fashion, with the construction of an artillery outpost known as
a firebase, which would later be given a name like "Firebase Bastogne" and
anchored by a battery of 105 howitzers along with a weapons platoon with
mortars and heavier machine guns.

This area differed from others we normally operated in due to the
fact that it was on fairly level ground as opposed to the hilltops in the
Central Highlands that we were used to. The old military axiom of whoever "holds the high ground" remains true to this day. The visual advantage
of a commanding view does provide reassurance and a psychological edge.
Flat as a pancake here.

The countryside here contained many old rubber plantations dating back to when Vietnam was a French colony. It was also uncomfortably
close to a network of infiltration trails the NVA used along the Cambodian
border. In a day or so, with the firebase completed, our company would
disappear into the countryside and operate under the protective umbrella
of those same 105s and mortars.

Complete darkness had enveloped the firebase when I hear a very
loud explosion coming from the edge of our perimeter.

I'm afraid I can't do better than that for a description without special effects. Insert your version of what an explosion sounds like and multiply it by ten.

Not knowing who, or for that matter, what, had triggered it, was unknown at this stage. A good guess would be NVA sappers.

We knew it was coming. Can't say it was a surprise. It was more a matter of how many and with what intensity.

They had been harassing us throughout the day as we helped fortify the firebase. Persistent small arms fire in our direction at various times had everyone on edge. First from one direction and then another. I wasn't overly concerned about an attack. In fact I thought they were crazy to try and engage us, a full Infantry Company backed up by 105 howitzers at arm's reach. Were they nuts? Had they no idea what we could counter with? We were all veterans at this point, and to be challenged in this way was not going to be good for those picking the fight.

Digging bunkers, trenches, and defensive positions. Filling and stacking sandbag on top of sandbag. Stringing rows of barbed wire. Claymore mines and booby traps set. Anyone trying to penetrate this perimeter would have their work cut out for them. Behind the barbed wire and assorted mines we had dug bunkers well protected with sandbags and firing slits for our machine guns. Behind our bunkers were the fortified 105 howitzers situated in the center of the firebase, each 105 in turn with its own ring of protective sandbags.

The NVA sappers chose the wrong entry point, the wire they snagged wasn't the barbed wire we had spent all day stringing.

No, it was a separate wire. It was a trip wire that led to our custom-made booby trap.

The "Widow Maker, Instantaneous" or just plain-old booby trap. Call it by whatever; it would be an IED, in today's lingo. It demonstrated its killing effectiveness once again. Made up with an arbitrary mixture of frags and Claymore minds strung together, there is zero delay once the circuit is tripped. A deadly cocktail of BB pellets and shrapnel followed.

A tremendous noise announced that someone had tripped it; then silence.

We waited a bit before responding, laying low in our bunkers, not replying with our weapons. No need to expose our position with all sorts of muzzle flashes just yet.

Immediately to our rear, with their barrels horizontal and parallel to the ground, the 105 howitzers commenced their firing.

In turns, their explosions followed almost immediately by the more massive explosion of the round itself exploding into the tree line, pulverizing trees not more than 100 yards to my front.

Any exposed life didn't stand a chance.

Firing anti-personnel Beehive rounds, each containing thousands of nail-like steel darts.

The devastation of the explosions taking place at the tree line was truly a spectacle to witness. I hunkered down and let my ears keep me posted as to the events. I didn't need my head to be taken off with some stray piece of shrapnel.

This continued for the better part of a half an hour before the 105s let up their pounding. Not a peep from the tree line. For good measure, we had the M79 grenade launchers lob intermittent shots into the tree line for another 10 to 15 minutes. This could be done with good effect because of their high trajectories and in a way so as to not reveal our position.

They ceased. The response from the tree line, again nothing. Quiet. Not a surprise given the intensity of firepower dished out.

The quiet remained throughout the night.

We waited for daylight to reveal what lay before us.

I get up in the morning these days and have on my iPad news feeds of all the major news outlets from around the world.

General news, science journals, sports, you name it, I'll scan them and focus my time ("focus" being the operative word as I approach my 70th birthday) to get to what will benefit me while trying to avoid the trash.

In that period described above, which took place in early 1968, the world's top newspapers all had on their respective front pages the following types of headlines:

"Tet Offensive launched in Vietnam throughout the country. All major towns and provincial capitals are being attacked in a surprise move by the NVA and Viet Cong with thousands of casualties."

The offensive lasted for almost a month and our outfit was involved in much of it. Going into Saigon and later up to Hue and Phu Bai in the north, I saw for myself the tremendous damage it caused.

From a military standpoint the NVA and Viet Cong suffered massive casualties. Yet from a PR standpoint it was a pivotal turning point, and a political victory on the part of the North Vietnamese.

The American perception of the war and its true scope took a pivotal shift at this time. The cost in lives, the length of the war, the continued demand for troops (already exceeding 500,000 American service men and women), the financial factors, and the stock political answers to these difficult questions, were no longer being bought by the American public.

Some of the images that remain with me are just like the iconic journalistic photos of the period:

- A South Vietnamese general putting a pistol to the head of a suspected Viet Cong in Saigon. The picture catches the impact of the bullet as it enters the Viet Cong's head.

- An outfit from our sister battalion landing on the roof of the American Embassy in Saigon to retake it from the Viet Cong.

- A Buddhist Monk in Saigon, sitting in the lotus position while a fellow monk pours gasoline on him. Set on fire, the burning monk enveloped in flames calmly remains seated, not moving or stirring from this horrific reality. Then he slowly toppled over to his death. This was done as a protest against the war.

- The immense casualties on all sides to retake the old imperial city of Hue. The Marines catching the brunt of that battle.

- Another casualty was many irreplaceable architectural features and buildings of that ancient city My Lai.

CHAPTER 31:

What's Your Sleep Number?

———◆———

TIME TO CALL IT A DAY AND SELECT A NIGHT LOCATION. Dusk is approaching and we are near the summit of a nameless hill, surrounded by many other nameless hills identified only by grid marks on a map. The elevation: always too high.

It could be raining. If not, the sweat from the day's exertion to get to where we are left us just as soaked. We are drenched in total and complete exhaustion. So happy to remove and set down our 60-pound rucksacks.

The platoon arranges itself in a loose defensive perimeter, often in vegetation so thick we have difficulty seeing the squad next to us. We set up our trip flares, Claymores, and booby traps.

Those essentials taken care of, it's time to break out the chow and savor a quiet meal, and coffee or hot chocolate, before hitting the sack. The day's light is fading fast and soon I'll be hard put to see my hand in front of my face.

Meal over, I undo the straps holding my bedroll located at the bottom of my rucksack.

Before laying out the bedroll, I scan for the all-important piece of ground that will be my bed and select it. When operating in the Central Highlands, finding a level spot was pretty well out of the question. The nagging aggravation of sleeping on less-than-level ground was an ongoing irritation that affected us all.

Other considerations for picking a piece of ground: You don't want to pick a spot near red ants, leeches, scorpions, centipedes, or snakes, to name some of the more undesirable sleeping companions. Not always avoidable, but we do our best. Liberal use of insect repellent for mosquitos is also advisable, and we always sleep with our clothes on, as exposing bare skin announces a buffet line for the above critters.

Having cleared one's spot with a machete or entrenching tool, it's time to lay out the bedroll.

Let me say that no matter how hard I try to clear a nice, smooth area, there's always a rock, stone, and/or twig poking me somewhere. Add to that a constant tug of gravity, an ever-present reminder that you're on an incline.

Back to setting up that "bed." First, my poncho, which I've folded to act as a ground sheet. Next, a camouflage blanket that serves as, well, the blanket. And that's it. Just those two items. No cushy air mattress or sleeping bag.

Should the rain be coming down hard, I would fold the poncho blanket around myself à la "bedroll burrito."

The pillow? I mastered a technique to sleep on my back with my head cradled in the helmet liner. With the hard ground, sleeping on one's side or stomach was out of the question.

My '16? Right beside me, the removable clip on bipod set to keep it above the dirt and ready for action.

Once asleep, I'd be cutting zzzzzzzz's like a baby. The day's exhaustion ensured that. The other factor was the need to be woken up twice at night to pull guard duty. Being stirred from a deep sleep is never pleasant and none of us ever got used to it. We rotated the guard times within the squad.

Guard duty required maintaining vigilance at our perimeter position. The darkness was often complete, though many areas had fireflies. I'd watch their light slowly fade in and out. They always provided me with a certain peace and comfort. They seemed unaffected by the surrounding death and destruction.

Dawn. As soon as first light permits, we would be up. Minimal talking, all done with whispers, as noise discipline is paramount. In no time my bedroll is gathered and secured to my rucksack. Breakfast is quietly eaten, C-ration cans are buried. Claymores, trip flares, and booby traps are gathered up in reverse of the previous evening, and stashed. We tidy up, leaving little sign of our presence.

An uneasy apprehension over the day's prospects creeps in. Never knowing what the day holds, but we're out here looking for trouble and it's all around us big time.

"Saddle up!" Yes, that's what we said. We put on our LBE (which looked like a toolbelt with suspenders, and held canteens, frags, bayonet, first-aid pouch, and ammo pouches or clips). Then we would put on the rucksack over it all.

We rarely spend the night in the same location. Each day has us expanding our range, forever on the move. Searching for NVA hidden out there somewhere; they in turn, were looking for us. We're aware of each other's presence, but who will be the first to see the other?

CHAPTER 32:

It's Time

———◆————

Chopper Assault

OUR "SLICK," A HUEY CHOPPER, THE ROTOR BLADES beginning their lazy rotations, now increasing along with the high-pitched whine of the turbine engine. Their ubiquitous sound is known to every Vietnam veteran.

Our outfit, Charlie Company 2, 502nd Infantry, First Brigade, 101st Airborne Division, is assembled on the tarmac. Two-hundred plus combat troops, give or take. Everybody's rucksack is loaded to the max with food, ammo, sundries, and water. We're heading out to the boonies on a search and destroy operation.

Somewhere in the Central Highlands, Gunships are "prepping" a mountaintop LZ for us, known only by its elevation and map coordinates.

Most of the troops are sitting or leaning against their "personal packages of torment," the rucksack. None of us are in any hurry to stand, to bear its weight and feel the pain and discomfort of the straps digging into our shoulders. My eyes are squinting to keep out the dust. My towel, normally around my neck, is draped over my '16, shielding it from that same dust.

We're all into our own thoughts.

Small talk, jokes, trash talk: All lessen considerably.

The previous day's memorial service held for those in our company is still fresh in our mind.

M16s fixed with a bayonet, planted into the earth with a helmet on top, spit-shined boots in front. All in a row, a final "formation of death" representing Troopers from our last operation.

Countless choppers seem to occupy the whole tarmac.

The pace of activity increases along with the noise, making any communication difficult without shouting.

Some Slicks are now easing into the air in a slow hover. Ascending, they arrange themselves in groups of three.

Our pilot, looking younger than me, flight helmet under his arm, has completed his exterior checklist. Donning his helmet he climbs into the cockpit and does a final check with the copilot.

A door gunner is on one side at the rear, the crew chief on the other. Each has an M60 machine gun to cover their side of the chopper. For now, the 60's point down, hanging loose in their slings, dangling in front of each gunner, while long belts of 7.62 ammo are arranged and tweaked to fit personal preferences.

Hand signals and looks from our squad leader are all that's needed to tell us it's our turn to board. Rucksacks on, hunched over, carefully avoiding the spinning rotor blades, we board.

Four to five fully loaded Troopers per Slick.

I triple-check to make sure my towel is protecting my '16 from the swirling dust; last thing I need is it to jam at this critical time.

We slide onto the floor of the chopper assuming an awkward seating position. The real seats, made of aluminum and webbing, are folded up and back out of the way, unable to be used with our oversized rucksacks. Pilot, copilot, door gunner, crew chief, four to five "packs" (us), we're set, let's go.

Liftoff.

The side doors on both sides will remain open throughout the flight. The rotor blades have reached the necessary RPMs, their iconic slapping sounds so familiar to all of us. We begin our ascent, most of us facing out the doors with legs dangling. No seats belts or pre-flight safety reviews.

Two other choppers swing beside us, forming our little group of three. We take our place in a long procession of other groups of three, stretching to the mountains on the horizon. One big, long, gaggle of deadly geese.

The rice paddies below are pockmarked with countless bomb craters marking past battles. It isn't long before they give way to slightly rolling hills. The heat and humidity of the ground is replaced with the welcome cooler temperature of our higher altitude. Cool enough for our door gunner to be wearing his field jacket. It's a small measure of comfort given where we're going.

Population centers have thinned to nothing with the approaching mountains. The darkness of the more heavily vegetated mountains with their triple-canopy jungle spreads out below us. This will be our home and hunting ground for the next month at least. Sparsely populated, virtually no roads or trails. Maybe some Montagnard tribesman, a predominant ethnic group differing from the Vietnamese.

Up ahead we can now see it. Our LZ and point of entry for the upcoming operation.

From a distance they appear like slow lazy dragon flies, armed helicopters (gunships) circling, banking, circling in slow revolutions. All the while laying down a blanket of destruction, their mini-guns shelling out 6,000 rounds/minute (not a typo). They seem so harmless at this range. Not enough for you? The whoosh as they let go with their rockets, a lethal mixture of Willie Peter (white phosphorus) and high explosive, repeatedly slamming the LZ. The intensity of their firepower negates any response.

The gunships now pull back and make way for our insertion, hanging back on the fringes should they be needed.

Tension is mounting. Eight of us hanging by a rotor shaft, thousands of feet in the air. Virtually no armor protecting the chopper; for us, none.

AKs can easily bring down a chopper. If they had their .51 caliber, they would have a field day. Anti-aircraft guns? Don't even want to think about it.

The banking, spiraling maneuver by the chopper and the resulting incline has me convinced the pilot is trying to dump us out the side. I have a death grip on the seat webbing, my other hand clutching my weapon, praying not to fall out. I feel we're flying sideways as I view the ground below.

No nice stewardess asking us to fasten our seatbelts here as we prepare for a landing.

Crew chief and door gunner now take hold of and position their '60s facing out. They check the belt feeds, and lock and load.

Depending on the direction of the wind and which side the '60 is on, jamming of the mechanism can result from the ejected casings flying back into the gun. One of those many little things to be aware of.

Here comes the LZ.

Slow motion replaced by fast motion, the ground rushes to meet us. Door gunners begin firing bursts into the tree line for cover. I pick out the random crack of an AK round going by. All this adding to the extra noise that has been pounding our ears on the trip here.

We're here.

Its nose rising slightly, our chopper slows to a hover. Gunner and crew chief lean out, checking the ground clearance for the pilot, at the same time frantically waving at us to jump out. The swirling dust at departure is now replaced with swirling twigs, leaves, branches, mixed with smoke from residual fires. Awkwardly we drop to the ground, making our exit. Mission accomplished, our now empty chopper rises slightly, and then banks, following the mountainside down at treetop height, picking up speed and then altitude.

It was a five or six foot jump to uneven terrain. I made it.

One by one, in rapid order, the choppers succeed in their mission of putting everyone safely down. Individual Troopers link with their squads, squads with platoons, platoons with the company. A defensive perimeter is established to assess the situation before setting out.

There had been some small-arms fire from a distance, but nothing of consequence. We're all here in one piece. That critical first step: a success.

The terrain on which we sit is scarred in the obscene way only explosives can do. Shrapnel in twisted, jagged pieces lies all over. A lingering smell from the explosives mixes with the smoke of burning vegetation ignited by the Willie Peter rockets. Pockets of grass fires burn themselves out.

The random pops and cracks of the exploding bamboo plants with their air chambers giving way mimic the cracks of AKs, keeping everyone on edge.

Time to melt into the Boonies and get lost, literally. We set off single file into the triple-layer canopy.

The racket, noise, gunfire, rockets, all replaced with silence.

It's an uneasy silence, though—one through which we constantly strain to pick out the sound of the unusual.

Soon our company will further disperse to platoons to maximize our coverage of our AO (area of operations—the designated territory on our maps to be searched out).

The group of two hundred or so has now been reduced to spread-out platoons and squads where just two or three of us are visible to each other. Though geographically not separated by great distances, given the rugged terrain it could take the better part of a day to link up should an ambush take place.

We are now in a world where the senses of smell and hearing replace sight as the dominant warning system.

Every day we'll extend our range. Every night we'll set up in a different night location. Let me repeat that, every night we set up perimeter at a different night location. We're not out here camping, digging in, and holding territory; no, we're always on the move. Patrolling, setting up ambush sites. Sometimes we spend more than a day to reach the summit of a hill, legs begging for relief from the constant weight on our backs.

We are ever on the move looking to engage the enemy, themselves dispersed in groups large and small in this same territory. The cat and mouse game has begun.

Before the month is out, some of us will be wounded, some dead. It's been that way in past operations and there is no reason to believe it will be different now.

Technology has made data-logging devices like Mapmyride/Google Maps common and now part of my daily routine. I'm now able to log/record walks, bike rides, and many other activities.

But I often find myself wondering how many steps, hill elevations, and distance traveled?

CHAPTER 33:
Do You Feel Lucky?

———◆——

DETECTIVE HARRY CALLAHAN, TALKING TO THE BAD GUY

I know what you're thinking. Did he fire six shots or only five? Well, to tell you the truth, in all this excitement I kind of lost track myself. But being as this is a .44 magnum, the most powerful handgun in the world, and would blow your head clean off, you've got to ask yourself one question. Do I feel lucky?

"Well, do ya, punk?" (yes, it's what was said in the movie)
–Clint Eastwood in *Dirty Harry*, 1971.

Whatever else you might have going for you in life, being lucky, call it what you will—blessed, having a good Guardian Angel—is key.

In the Infantry in particular, with the opposing side having killing you as their sole mission, a bit or lot of luck is critical. Goes without saying.

I was about 10 or 11, checking out the local gravel pit.

Standing on top, right by the edge. Below me a giant excavator was taking monster bites from the earth over fifty feet below me.

Whoomp! The earth dropped out from under me, and in an instant I found myself half buried in sand looking up at the bucket that a second ago was below me.

I scampered out, unhurt! The excavator operator was equally stunned by my dumb luck. But luck just the same.

Riding as a passenger in my brother's car. I saw it coming, and I don't know how he didn't.

My brother proceeds to make a left-hand turn, and the oncoming vehicle T-bones my passenger-side door. A witness later told me my head shattered the glass on the door.

I had to climb through the crumbled door to make my exit. Yet no cuts or bruises. I told the medics treating me I felt like an elephant had stepped on my rib cage. It felt that way for a week.

Lucky indeed!

Either way, luck, and lots of it, is what you want if you're going to be with an Infantry outfit, or any type of fighting outfit.

Naturally accident prone? Find another line of work.

When I was with the 82nd airborne Stateside we found ourselves playing war games in Pennsylvania. Lunch time, seated on a mountainside chowing down and watching some National Guard jets make dives in simulated bombing runs. One jet roars down into a steep dive. Lower and lower he goes, we wait and watch for him to pull up. Never happened. He drilled that jet into the ground. My spoon-stopper in mid-bite as I watched the huge fireball. Real bad luck! Not even a combat zone.

Firebase Bastogne, a "cherry" replacement was set to join our company, about to step off the chopper. A sniper round caught him in the head, killing him instantly. Potentially he might have been the best Trooper going. But lucky, no. You need both.

I was about to board a chopper, and then I was waved off to avoid overcrowding. The chopper lifted off, lost RPMs, and crashed! A similar event happened another time.

Was I lucky? You bet.

Lieutenant C., unaware of the faulty frag with a broken handle, went to dispose of it, and it exploded, blowing off his hand. Very unlucky!

A round hit the helmet of my squad leader, most definitely too close. Extremely lucky.

About to join my new unit in Chu Lai, I was told I was lucky to be assigned to Charlie Company. They're known to have fewer Troopers killed than Alpha or Bravo companies (gee, thanks!).

They were right: It was lucky in that respect.

I was out in the open, at the edge of the firebase perimeter, filling my canteens from a large rubber water bladder that the Chinook chopper had just delivered. Hooking onto the empty one, the big Chinook was slowly lumbering up, twin rotors kicking up huge clouds of dust in all directions.

It was at this moment that AK rounds by the dozen begin cracking all around me. The Chinook immediately cut the quick release, dropping the water bladder, hoping to crank up some speed and get the heck out of there.

Me, off like a jackrabbit, setting yet another personal best for the 50-yard dash, leaping behind the cover of sandbags ringing a 105 howitzer, AK rounds chasing me the whole way. The Chinook no doubt picked up a few holes, but made good his getaway.

We were both very lucky.

In Chapter 3, I mentioned my third parachute jump in Jump School, which almost cost me my life.

Just plain (dumb) good luck.

An NVA soldier who put a "burst" in my Rucksack, missing me by millimeters. So very lucky!

My platoon Sergeant F., well into his second tour, took a round to the chest. Killed him, they put him in a body bag, zipped it up—goodbye. But wait a minute! Movement was detected from the bag. Miraculously, he was alive! He went on to recover and added to his accumulations, numerous medals, and decorations and completed a full career in the Army. We all knew he was a Hard-Core dude, and this merely confirmed it.

Can't ask for more luck than that!

So, before you join that fight, or your think yourself a badass, you've got to ask yourself one question. Do I feel Lucky?...Well, do ya, punk?

CHAPTER 34:

Logging

———————◆———————

Da Nang

THE ALTITUDE AT WHICH WE CAME ACROSS THIS LOG-
ging operation was bizarre indeed. We were way up in the mountains of
neighboring Da Nang. Complicating the puzzle was the massive size of the
trees. We wondered how they could even be transported with no roads to
be seen

The terrain was steep. The fact that no machinery could be seen
added to the mystery.

No machinery, no access, no people to give us the answers.

Who Needs a Chainsaw?

Many times found us in situations with trees were too large to cut
down using our standard method, hacking away with machetes. This might
be required to make access for incoming resupply choppers.

A rather novel method was devised by our platoon Sergeant, until
one day it proved too hazardous to one's health. It went something like this.

Chop a notch near the base of the tree that required relocating, about
the size of a softball.

Take a frag (fragmentation grenade), wedge it tightly into the notch,
and yell "Fire in the hole!" Pull the pin, and then run like hell!

Extremely crazy, dangerous, even borderline insane, when you think about it.

Often some of us in close proximity weren't aware of the impending explosion. The "Fire in the hole" would be shouted but we lacked the necessary time to complete the "run like hell" part of the sequence. This creative logging system proved effective for a while. Eventually three of our guys were wounded and required medical evacuation as a result of this method of clearing trees.

Orders were issued from the powers that be. This novel way of tree removal was to cease immediately!

And it did stop, for the most part. Still, sometimes a bit of C4 (plastic explosive) would find its way into one or another more stubborn tree.

"Fire in the hole!" The brute force logging method

We're on our way to a hilltop for a combat assault. Dense jungle growth needed removal to provide clearance for the choppers to drop off the troops.

We had the solution for that.

We had our buddies from the air force in Jets make a few passes with 500-pound bombs. Guaranteed to open up a clearing! Want something bigger? The 2,000-pound blockbuster baby could relocate a whole mountain top. If a few enemy bunkers were destroyed in the process, hey, extra points were given.

Who Needs an Axe?

The firefight over, the NVA had withdrawn. We were going over the field of battle looking for bodies and weapons. Few bodies, many blood trails.

Suddenly a tree (about 10 inches in diameter) took this moment to slowly topple over. T-i-m-b-e-r!!

I remember watching the tree as it fell and marveled at the quantity of ammo needed to achieve that effect.

Against all odds it had remained perfectly upright all this time. Its base had been totally shredded by our M60 machine gunner. In the heat of the battle, the gunner—adrenaline going full bore—had been laying down lead with little regard to his aim. It demonstrated the hitting power of those 7.62 rounds if nothing else. It chewed through that tree like a beaver with steel teeth.

Weed Wacker/Chopper

He was badly wounded.

The dense jungle, insanely tall trees, all made us doubt if we could get him out in time, or out at all.

With trees in excess of 100 feet, we spotted an opening that just—and I do say just—might allow a chopper to hover below the tree line. From there an attempt could be made to lower a stretcher on a winch and haul our wounded buddy up.

An extremely risky venture, but the dustoff (ambulance chopper) pilot was game to give it a shot.

We popped yellow smoke. It billowed out and we crossed our fingers hoping the pilot could see the tiny opening we picked out. He did, and began a slow vertical descent into the opening.

The circumference of the opening was not much beyond the reach of the whirling blades. He kept descending until the rotor blades were just below the tree tops. Then he held his position.

Even if nothing else was going on, at this stage alone the chopper was in great danger. The "prop wash" had the surrounding trees/branches waving in chaotic motion. At any moment it could be game over. A loose branch sucked into the blades would have ended the whole matter.

There was that aspect to the whole thing.

What about NVA in the vicinity?

Sure, the firefight was over and we had more or less secured the area. Still, the target presented by an unarmed chopper with its big red ambulance cross painted on the underside made it a sniper's dream.

The pilot and medics had to keep those thoughts away as they slowly lowered the stretcher, secured the wounded soldier, and raised him back up again.

Miraculously, all went well! I can't say enough about the courage of those dustoff pilots and crews. Always unarmed and ready to risk their lives to save others.

It could easily have gone the other way with the chopper becoming a large weed whacker, resulting in the death of the crew and some of us underneath.

Tetrachlorodibenzodioxin

Get your chemistry books out kids!

Actually there's no need. The critical part of the above compound are the last six letters, dioxin, aka Agent Orange.

A truly deadly class of chemicals linked to many forms of cancer and birth defects, and with side effects too numerous to mention here. If you want more detail to ruin your day, Google "Agent Orange" and pages of its side effects and pictures of poor souls afflicted by its results can be seen.

It's tragic to reflect that killing chemicals such as these were created by well-intentioned people for use in totally unrelated purposes. In this case, mostly by Monsanto and Dow Chemical. Considered an effective way to clear large area of trees/foliage, huge amounts (not just thousands, but millions of gallons) of the defoliant known as Agent Orange were sprayed over vast portions of Vietnam by a variety of aircraft.

Thought to be relatively safe at the time, it proved to be an effective killer on levels way beyond those intended.

The chemicals used in Agent Orange were later discovered to be extremely toxic. Not only were the trees killed but also the water and groundcover of all kinds. Hey! We didn't stop there. Let's kill the crops, too! In a misguided attempt to deprive the enemy of food supplies, many acres of rice paddies were destroyed by this chemical, and the groundwater was poisoned for years to come. It was later discovered that many innocent farmers suffered/starved from these actions, but few of the enemy.

Laos and Cambodia, neighboring counties of Vietnam, were also doused with large amounts of this chemical for many of the same reasons.

Many Vietnam Veterans were later to die, and others continue to be afflicted by this form of chemical warfare. Countless civilians in that region of Southeast Asia suffered the same fate with even fewer resources.

CHAPTER 35:

Sappers, Continued

THE NIGHT REMAINED TENSE, BUT NO FURTHER ACTIV-
ity followed since we ceased firing the 105s, and M-79s.

Daylight came and it was time to see what sort of damage we had inflicted.

Two dead NVA lay where the initial explosion of our booby trap displayed its lethal result. Their AK's never fired a shot. Their explosives, which were to be used to provide a penetration point into our perimeter, were neutralized.

My attention turned to the tree line just past the perimeter. Our platoon was keen to sweep the area to see what damage the 105s had inflicted. The massive firepower that hammered that area the night before left us secure enough to venture out with little fear of counterfire.

But then a very strange development took place. The firebase we spent the whole day setting up and fortifying was now ordered to be dismantled. As in immediately.

What the hell is going on? Normally a firebase of this size would be utilized for a month or more.

We were later informed that what was to become known as the "Tet Offensive" was underway in full force. While the Offensive was happening throughout Vietnam, the bulk of the fighting was taking place in all major towns and cities. We were ordered to Saigon, which was in the midst of a fierce battle. We were being mobilized and transported as reinforcements.

This was just like when the circus comes to town with the big tent and rides taking days to assemble, and then magically disappears the day after closing.

With the pace of choppers coming and going, the artillery and heavier loads were rapidly being drawn down.

The growing void at the center was starting to impact the sense of security I possessed earlier in the morning. I kept a wary eye directed at the tree line. Could remnants or reinforcements be massing to strike in our weakened position? My unease was made worse with random grass fires that had flared up from the artillery fire. The smoke and growing intensity of the flames was quietly making their way in the direction of rucksacks containing a fair bit of ammo. It would not have been a good scenario if the rucksacks caught fire.

Choppers continued coming in to pull out the 105s, carried in slings below them. Sandbags were busted and emptied and bunkers filled in and destroyed.

Next, we, in groups of four per chopper load, were transported to a staging area where larger aircraft waited to fly us to Saigon.

The feeling that comes from strength in numbers was lessened as those numbers declined.

About this time someone calls my name and asks if I want to check out one of the dead g**ks, whose head was lopped off and now sits on a pole. No thanks, was my reply. That kind of creative extracurricular activity ain't my style.

Mutilation of bodies was no big surprise. As a rule we didn't go out of our way to practice it, but it does happen in various forms by both sides. Some of it is very obscene in every sense of the word.

The brass in the rear area got wind of it and word came down for us to cut (no pun intended) it out.

I was on one of the last loads to be extracted from the firebase. None too soon, with that grass fire licking its way ever closer, a decapitated head on a stake not far away, and eerie silence from the tree line. Get me out of here.

Our chopper slowly lifts and the new old firebase grows smaller as we gain altitude. I am disappointed by not being able to sweep the tree line and check for bodies. Less for the bodies themselves than for a possible cool war souvenir. A pistol or bayonet maybe, something I could take with me.

We disembark at an airstrip swarming with aircraft of every description. Large groups of troops are assembling and boarding C-130 troop transport planes for Saigon.

Still somewhat gung ho at the time, I was kind of looking forward to some city fighting where one could actually see where they're shooting at and get out of those claustrophobic Boonies.

On to Saigon.

CHAPTER 36:
Top Chef

———◆———

Hell's Kitchen

ONE CAN'T GET TOO FAR IN TALKING ABOUT THE ARMY without discussing its fine cuisine (wishful thinking). The old axiom that an army runs on its stomach has never been more true.

Logistics and supply is not a sexy topic when discussing military undertakings, but let me tell you, troops missing a few meals is a recipe for mutiny in no time flat.

Next time you see pictures of some nifty-looking army in a third world country being paid next to nothing, small wonder they're taking bribes and shaking down whoever may be around them.

No pay, no food, no discipline. Basically just a lot of grumpy people running around with guns. Doesn't make for a good combo.

The meals we had in the mess hall Stateside were adequate, and I don't really recall anything I'd turn down. Even the infamous "chipped beef on toast" (aka "s**t on a shingle") was never declined; in fact, I sort of liked it. My main complaint was due to the fact that we weren't allowed to go back for seconds. The exception was the milk dispenser. One spigot for white milk, one for chocolate milk. I would load up on chocolate milk. Yum!

Of course we always had the option of eating off-post or doing something like ordering pizza on weekends.

When I was in the 82nd Airborne Division Stateside, we would sometimes go out to the field and play war games. That was my first exposure to C-rations, which would become the mainstay of our meals in Vietnam.

I'll tell you I wasn't impressed. Primarily because we would eat them cold and my chef skills in their preparation was lacking at the time. I was not a fan of the canned bread or many of the other meals.

Below I reflect on some of the more memorable eating experiences. These are exceptions, though. Mostly it was Cs and more Cs.

Phan Rang

Let me begin with Thanksgiving meal in Phan Rang. Phan Rang is in a nice location situated on coastal Vietnam by the South China Sea. Initially it served as the main rear-area base camp for the First Brigade of the 101st Airborne Division. As rear areas go it was very safe. We shared it with a division of Troopers from the Republic of Korea. Additionally, a squadron of Australian Canberra Bombers were stationed there.

We had returned to Phan Rang after pulling search-and-destroy operations further north in Chu Lai. The peaceful vibe surrounding Phan Rang was a relaxing interlude from the constant stress in the Boonies. Safer than Stateside. We're on stand down for four days, and then back out to the Boonies for a month or so.

The cooks had pulled out all the stops and prepared a super meal along the lines of a traditional Thanksgiving meal. I can't remember the specifics other than lots of good food. The fact that it was such a contrast from our day-to-day chow made it pop all the more. We pigged out big time that day and everyone had a smile on their face. The one negative was some of us had to do the dishes. Yes. My only time for KP duty in 'Nam.

The meal has been prepared in what's known as a field kitchen, which made cleanup more work. I was going to provide the details but it would activate my "KP-PTSD" and give me nightmares of cleaning endless stacks of dishes, forks and knives, and pot and pans that still haunt me from my days in training.

But all in all a great day!

Da Nang

We had concluded an operation and were exiting the Boonies in a manner out of the ordinary. Usually we would be on some mountaintop to be picked up by choppers and returned to the rear area. Being near the coast by Da Nang, it was decided that we could hump out to Highway 1 (the coastal highway). And make our way to the rear area from there.

As a treat we were to be greeted and served a hot meal courtesy of the Marines. Wow! Platoon by platoon, single file, we waited our turns for security purposes. I was still in the undergrowth drooling my way closer to the chow trucks. Word was passed back that cake was included in the meal. Cake! I can't get there soon enough!

BOOOM !! Nooooo! Explosion. Dust and dirt rain down.

A Deuce supply half-truck just hit a mine, blowing off a front wheel! The driver was wounded but not killed.

Enough about the trivia. What about my chow! Let's get our priorities straight here!

Eventually I find my way to the front. All was not lost. Most of the food survived. The cake had a fine layer of dust on the icing but was basically intact. No big deal, tasted super!

Christmas Meal

A story in itself, which appears in Chapter 44.

Corned Beef Hash

On patrol, we came across an abandoned firebase. It had belonged to one of our units and they would receive a part of their rations in larger bulk containers. One of these half-opened gallon-sized containers still had a good amount of corned beef hash in it. That wasn't an item found on our daily menu.

We removed a layer of ants from the top portion and the rest smelled halfway OK. We served it up, and it disappeared quicker than it was found. Can't let these gourmet treats go by the wayside.

Pig Roast

We had been in a recent firefight. Dead bodies were still within view, taking the edge off my appetite.

That didn't deter one of our guys from bayoneting one of the now homeless pigs in the vicinity. All the squealing from the pig lessened my appetite even more. An attempt was made to cook it on a spit but he didn't really have the time needed to turn it into a five-star meal. We had to move on. I heard it wasn't all that tasty.

Spoils of War

Precious few. Way out in the Boonies, the few farming hooches we'd encountered didn't provide much in the way of plunder. However, I did discover a sealed can of cookies that I considered taking. Can't remember how they tasted, so maybe I didn't take it?

CHAPTER 37:

Fort Dix

OVER TWO MONTHS HAVE PASSED SINCE MY ENLIST-
ment in Detroit. Fall is here, and the more northern climate will makes this
part of my training a little chillier. At one point I remember bivouacking in
our pup tents and waking to a layer of snow.

To recap, I'm here to take Advanced Infantry training for two months
as a necessary prerequisite for Officers Candidate School. Something I
qualified for while in Basic Training, this came about by taking routine
tests given to us in Basic.

I've rejoined my buddies from Basic Training for this next step in
what has become a detour from my initial enlistment track (working with
cryptographic machines).

I'm still feeling lukewarm about this whole OCS deal, and less than a
week into training leaves me even less enthusiastic.

The barracks were a step up from the ones we had in Basic, but that's
about it. The training itself was much like that in Basic. The big difference
being that the harassment from the Drill Sergeant has been ratcheted up a
notch. The whole idea is to harass the hell out of us and weed out those of
us who aren't OCS material.

Part of the training had us qualify on additional weapons: the 1911
.45 pistol and the M60 machine gun. I admit having fun firing the .50 caliber machine gun. I was a lousy shot with the .45 (most of us were) but a

qualified expert on the M60 machine gun. Who doesn't like firing bursts on full automatic at barrels staged every 200, 400, and 600 yards?

The rest of it, though—the drills, marching, PT, KP, inspections and more inspections, and being hassled for trivial matters—left me having what my Drill Sergeant referred to as a "bad attitude." I was accused of having a bad attitude so much that it began to feel like part of my name. I'll admit that I did not exhibit the proper military bearing. At that time in the Army I had not yet learned how to "play the game." and the chip on my shoulder resulted in my being volunteered on numerous occasions for KP.

You rise at 0300 to report to the Mess Sergeant to be assigned to one of the following choice positions: Pots and pans, some big enough to serve as Hot tubs. Dishes and Trays, you guessed it, washing and cleaning tons of dishes/cutlery. Dining room orderly, glorified bus boy. Floors were waxed and buffed after every meal, inside and outside (shipping and receiving).

This was done in a mess hall that would accommodate 200 GIs at a meal three times a day.

The Mess Sergeant could have been a copy of Chef Ramsay from the TV reality show "Hell's Kitchen." He used the same language, and the slightest infraction would have me redoing all 200 dishes or whatever, if it wasn't done to his standards.

The day normally ended about 10 PM. You bet I had a bad attitude.

About six to seven weeks into our training, we went before a review board of three officers for an individual evaluation to determine whether or not to let us advance to Officers Candidate School.

Into the room I go.

The three officers seated before me (and not chosen for their sense of humor) ask me a few basic questions on my reasons for wanting to become an officer. It would be fair to say that I didn't do the best job of selling myself. To top it off, some of my "bad attitude" may have presented itself.

Thumbs down.

No reason is given. Can't say I was surprised.

The only bummer is all my buddies have passed their evaluations and will be moving on without me to OCS.

Soon the two months of training is complete, and at this stage I've indirectly acquired an MOS (military occupation specialty) of Infantry by default. Not my first choice by a long shot.

As an enlistee I opt to go back to my enlistment choice (working with cryptographic machines). Which by rights was mine.

Oops! They say. That choice is now denied me as it requires a Top Secret security clearance and as a Canadian with a Green Card I cannot get that clearance! Whaaat! Why wasn't I told that at the time I enlisted? (Had I known then and there, I should have been allowed to proceed with my enlistment choice or released from the service without penalty.)

I was a victim of the old bait and switch.

All is not lost, I'm told; we can offer you an MOS as a telephone lineman.

I'll take it. Good, they say. Report tomorrow for orders to go to the lineman school in Fort Huachuca, Arizona.

Sounds neat, I thought. I've never been to Arizona, and was looking forward to the Southwest.

Tomorrow comes. I'm in formation and I hear my name called along with two Mexicans and a Samoan.

We fall out of formation and are told that we cannot go to Ft. Huachuca, Arizona because that MOS also requires a security clearance. Well now my bad attitude is really beginning to show, along with much frustration.

Further options are offered me—cook, truck driver (me? A truck driver!) or mechanic. Jobs where we won't be a threat to national security.

Totally frustrated and fed up with all the training BS, I decided no. Since I'm already qualified as Infantry, just let me go to Jump School so I can be a Paratrooper, and once my three years are up, I'm out of there and back to the bank. Not being too concerned that Vietnam was ramping up big time and odds were I'd soon end up there.

No big deal, how bad could it be? That was my thinking then. After all, the bad stuff only happens to the other guy.

One last hurdle before Jump School. I had to pass a quick physical.

The doctor gave me a minor going over, a few deep knee bends, nothing too heavy duty. He did take the time to point out that my extreme short-sightedness at the time, 20/400, could easily exclude me from any non-combat arms duty. He was giving me a chance to be excluded from any combat position.

Still not fazed by future prospects, I convince him I want to move on.

No, I'm fine, let me go on to Jump School, I tell him. Which is what he did.

CHAPTER 38:
Civilian to G.I.

———◆———

THE TRAIN RIDE TOOK US TO FORT KNOX, KENTUCKY.
Not too exciting a ride, as I recall.

It's about a day's ride south of Detroit, and once we arrived, the little I remembered the short week there was very elementary. Lots of greasy hairstyles shorn off like so many sheep at an Australian sheep-shearing station. Or if you were a Brother, your 'Fro' went just as fast. From all walks of life, some with better hygiene than others. Our new cue bald heads revealed some pretty nasty head sores on some of the recruits. For them, Basic Training meant learning basic hygiene never taught at home.

Next, gone went our civvies and we were given uniforms. The fatigues issued were olive drab in color (fancy camouflaged uniforms were a long ways off and didn't really come on the scene until long after I left the service), and made of a heavy denim material unlike the jungle fatigues we were to wear in Vietnam. Heavy black boots, steel pot and liner. Class A khaki made the more formal wear. How to stand in formation, marching, how to address the drill sergeants, the very basics given us here.

All of us were given a variety of aptitude tests, the results of which were to come into play once I got into Basic Training.

All of the above took place over a week's time. The real training began with Basic Training.

The Army, Marines, Air Force, and Navy all have their own version, which is similar in many respects. They differ somewhat in length and severity.

Basic Training

From Fort Knox, Kentucky it was off to Basic Training, which for me took place at Fort Campbell, Kentucky. It's a two-month period of training that is pretty well the entry point for every soldier.

During that period of time we're all taught, well, the basics of soldiering.

Our Drill Instructors were very good at doing the usual Drill Instructor things: letting us know what low lives we were and reminding us that we're just GIs (Government Issue) with no rights and our ass now belonged to Uncle Sam.

Doing tons of push-ups for every little infraction, real or imagined. Discipline, obeying orders, big points were given for that. Opinions, thinking, suggestions on how do things better will find one doing more push-ups.

Marching, how to stand in formation, making beds to military standards, how to dress the military way, how to do KP and clean lots and lots of dishes, pots and pans, mopping of floors. Let's not forget scrubbing down latrines.

A word about our latrines.

Our barracks were the old two-story type constructed of wood left over from World War II, and the crappers in the latrines were all nicely lined up in a row, but without any dividers or separations of any kind from each other! Please! Can't we have some privacy here?

The newer concrete barracks I was to be housed in later training were to have private crappers with dividers. A little more civilized. In any event, privacy is a rare commodity in the military.

Back to training. We were issued M14s as the standard military rifle then. It was the successor to the M1 used in World War II and predated the M16 which I was to use in Vietnam. Heavier than the '16 and used heavier ammo, too.

Weapons are another item the Army loves to make you clean to the nth degree. Much time was spent cleaning, dismantling, reassembling, and starting all over again.

We marched to the rifle range and learned the fundamentals of firing, zeroing one's weapon, different firing stances, and firing at targets from a variety of distances, and got graded accordingly. In Basic Training, the M-14 was the only weapon we qualified on. Qualification on a variety of other weapons came about in later training.

How to toss a frag along with a variety of other grenades (smoke, CS-gas [military grade tear gas], and Willie Peter [white phosphorous]) was touched on.

Lots of physical training. Marching, jogging, all of which was expected and didn't faze me much. I had been a distance runner in school and looked upon the whole thing as a challenge.

During basic training I formed a friendship with about 5 or 6 fellow trainees. We hung around together and as it turned out the aptitude tests we had taken in the first week in Fort Knox, Kentucky qualified us for OCS (Officers Candidates School).

OCS is one of the main means by which the Army trains soldiers to become officers. ROTC (Reserve Officers Training Corps and West Point are a couple of others.)

This training is composed of eight weeks of AIT (Advanced Infantry Training) as a prerequisite. Once completed, we would proceed to Officer Candidate School, which is comprised of six more months of training. Assuming all went well, graduates are then commissioned with the rank of Second Lieutenant, the entry officer rank in the Army.

I was lukewarm on the whole idea. Yes, being an officer has more privileges, benefits, and the like, but I saw it more as a career track for those wanting to pursue the Army as a profession. That conflicted with my enlistment choice and university track I had in mind for myself.

As I remember, the collective thinking with my buddies won out, and we all agreed to give this Officer Candidate School thing a try.

Our eight weeks of Basic Training successfully completed, we kissed all that harassment goodbye and went off on leave to our respective homes to rejoin later at Fort Dix, New Jersey for AIT.

CHAPTER 39:

The Rucksack

---◆---

IT'S A GYM, PHARMACY, PANTRY, CLOSET, ARMORY, recliner, firing cover, stress test, and then some. Every Trooper's personal package of torment.

Unlike the Mickey Mouse day pack we used Stateside when playing war games in the field with the 82nd Airborne Division, the rucksack was a serious step up in capacity.

Empty, it looks unimposing. But it's what goes in, on, and around it that leads to all sort of moaning and groaning.

With a basic aluminum frame, web backing, and shoulder straps, the rucksack and side pouches are secured to the top of the frame, leaving space on the bottom for the bedroll (except for some of the guys in the 327 who put their bedroll on top—I don't know why they did that). The bedroll was simplicity itself. Poncho and poncho liner rolled and secured to the bottom of the frame.

One of the first things needed is additional padding for the shoulder straps. Most of us used foam rubber and taped it on the shoulder straps to lessen the digging of the straps into our shoulders.

Empty, it doesn't look too imposing for an item that can cause such pain. Fully loaded it could easily top 60 pounds. It was so heavy and awkward to hoist on one's shoulder, most of us wouldn't bother expending the effort and energy attempting to put it on while standing.

In addition to the rucksack, we had what was called the LBE (load bearing equipment), which was a heavy-duty web belt with equally heavy duty suspenders. From the LBE hung ammo pouches, canteens, first-aid pouch, smoke grenade, knife/bayonet, and maybe a .45. The LBE was a tidy bit of weight in its own right.

The preferred method to shoulder the rucksack would be to have it on the ground, slide up to it backwards, and loop the shoulder straps through your arms.

Now do a slow awkward roll onto one's knees, and then stand up. Whew!

So what goodies went inside? Well, mostly food, ammo, and water.

We'd each be given a case of C-rations that arrive in a large cardboard box. One case of Cs contains twelve different meals. Each meal in turn is in its own box, mostly in cans of two or three different sizes.

We could keep, trade, or chuck whichever meals we desired. It was up to us. That one case was to last four days. I pretty well kept them all. Breaking open the cardboard box, we'd remove all the cans and stuff them in the rucksack. At times we were given supplementary meals known as LRRPs, yummy and much-prized freeze-dried meals, a new concept then. They were lighter but more bulky.

Sundries were comprised of candy, cigarettes, heating tabs to cook the Cs, stationery, soap, shaving gear. Malaria pills, halazone, water purification tablets, and bottles of insect repellant made up the medicine cabinet.

The weight is—have your calculator handy!

Let's start with the C-ration box, which is itself over 20 pounds. Put that in your calculator memory for now.

Four or five canteens of water, the two that I mentioned on the LBE and the other two or three on the rucksack. Four canteens, that's one gallon, which equals eight pounds. Into the calculator; now we have 28 pounds. Wow! Almost 30 pounds and we haven't even started!

Now I said four or five canteens, but it you want more, feel free, it's your choice. But as a practical matter four or five work even though it never seems enough and one's thirst is never satisfied. You learn to sip, not guzzle! If you want to pack more, help yourself.

Next, ammo. As a rifleman with the M16, itself about four pounds empty, that'll put you at 32 pounds now. The '16 ammo, a minimum of

400 rounds in 20 clips of 19 to 20 rounds each, stuffed in ammo pouches, and bandoliers: add 15 pounds into the calculator, now at 47 pounds. Four frags and one Willie Peter grenade add 5 pounds, bringing the running total up to 52 pounds.

Machete and entrenching tool are good for 6 pounds, bringing it to 58 pounds. Claymore mine, bed roll, helmet, maybe a LAW (light antitank weapon): 10 more pounds. The calculator says 68 pounds. Tired yet?

Wait…there's more! You have to help the M60 gunner carry some of his ammo. One 100-round link is 8 pounds. I'll give you just one. Making for a total of 76 pounds.

Hold it! Can't run out there naked. Shirt, pants, two pairs of socks, and jungle boots. That's good for another 5 pounds easily. We now tip the scales at 81 pounds.

Remember, you never really want to run out of water or ammo. Add as much as you want, but just remember that it's all yours to carry. What about Flak Jackets? Rudimentary at the time, and only seen at firebases, by those in convoys, and at the rear area. We never use any. Body armor? Not yet on the scene.

Now, we're in the Central Highlands. We'll be going uphill all day, maybe more than one day. Even without weight of any kind, the heat, breaking brush, no trails, and the climbing has us pouring sweat. Going downhill is not much better. It's like doing leg squats. Always and ever on the move, no two nights in the same location.

Add to that the fact that we remained in the Boonies on average a month at a time!

Too light for you, want more? The above are the lightest packs carried by our Troops in the Boonies. The heaviest are carried by the machine gunner. Packing the M60 machine gun, that alone is 24 pounds empty! In addition mentioned so far, he's draped in 100-rounds links of ammo. Again, at 8 pounds per link.

For the radio telephone operator (RTO), the radio alone is over 20 pounds. This was before the miracle of miniaturization and microchips. Add a couple of spare batteries and he's topped at 25 pounds before even tying his boots.

If you carried the M79 grenade launcher, as I did during my initial three months or so, that entailed lots of weight. My ammo alone weighed

25 to 30 pounds at a minimum. Not just heavy, but the rounds were bulky as can be.

Looking back on it now, while recently lifting a 60-pound bag of Quikcrete cement at Home Depot, I just don't know how we managed.

So do that, people: Grab a backpack and go to Lowes/Home Depot.

Buy and toss that 60-pounds Quikcrete cement into your backpack. Carry it around all day, and then sit down and read the above for a real sense of our daily torment.

CHAPTER 40:

Bamboo

———◆◆———

I LOVE BAMBOO. AT HOME, WE DIDN'T REALLY HAVE much of the type we came across in Vietnam.

The two small bamboo plants in my yard at home are tiny by comparison.

Hawaii has some bamboo groves that are more in line with what we encountered in Vietnam. Seventy-plus feet of height. Large-diameter stems, tall as trees though it's actually classed as a grass. Very versatile, bamboo has many uses: baskets, scaffolding, water piping, containers, on and on.

But in Vietnam…punji stakes!!! They're everywhere!! The vast majority are made from bamboo. They make the perfect poor man's bobby trap. Readily available in all parts of the country. Sharpened to a point and implanted in the ground at various angles. In every configuration, along trails, in pits, tunnels, as parts of traps. Some old-aged and blackened, dating back to the time when Vietnam was a French colony. Others, virtually new, green, and sharpened as if done yesterday, which they could well have been.

Sometimes we'll see a few, but more often dozens. I've come across whole fields of them. They could be cleverly concealed, most times easily visible.

The points are often covered in a feces or some nasty contaminant to ensure infection for those unlucky enough to stumble into them. In the tropics, small infections lead to big problems very fast.

I never stepped on any myself, though one time when walking through heavy brush, a thorn on a bamboo twig was released as if on the end of spring steel. The twig/thorn slashed through my thigh and gave me a nasty cut.

How it didn't become infected I'll never know.

Bao Loc

Our squad is setting out for patrol. We had a vague goal to locate a trail that was shown on our map. Fat chance, was my thought. We haven't seen anything resembling a trail for days; breaking brush had been the norm. The vegetation in this area was incredibly dense, more so than normal. Off we went. LBE and full ammo, leaving our rucksacks back with the platoon.

An hour into the patrol found us in the midst of a large bamboo grove. And a beautiful grove it was. Large, tall, stand-alone, nicely spaced apart, which made our travel through them somewhat quiet. But not that quiet. The ground was covered with a thick carpet of dried, crunchy, crispy bamboo leaves. Yes, it was like walking in a bowl of Rice Crispies and twice as noisy.

The two or three Troopers in front of me came to a sudden freeze, indicating with the slightest motion that something was up.

No need to explain. My thumb, already on the safety of my '16, is now extra ready to ease it to full auto. Single file, we proceed forward.

The all-out automatic weapons fire I'm waiting for doesn't materialize.

Given how exposed we are, I relax somewhat. Here and there I notice many tunnel entrances and other fortifications as we continue to what would be the "front" entrance to the complex.

It was a well-used trail disguised with some of the best booby traps I've ever seen. Bomb fuses and other explosive devices very cleverly concealed.

Still no sign of anyone?? Many bloody bandages lay scattered about. What's up?

Turns out that we had come across a large NVA field hospital. The majority of it was underground and barely visible.

Our point man had heard medical personnel and wounded evacuating as we made our way from the back door, so to speak. They must have had advance notice of our arrival to evacuate in time.

With just about a dozen of us, we wasted no time in radioing for help and after a tense hour of waiting, the rest of the company linked up.

Time to take stock of what we had. It was big. We had stumbled upon a large NVA M.A.S.H. hospital. Extensive tunnels systems and underground rooms made up the complex. Many of the tunnels were disguised with bobby traps in hidden locations.

It was large enough that a command decision was made for choppers to fly in special cratering charges. These forty-pound tubes of solid explosives were wired by the CE to collapse the main entrances and operating rooms and various chambers.

The complex was so big that we remained in that area two or three days to complete the job. Some large explosions for sure, but detonated underground so not much in the way of visual fireworks.

I was glad to finally leave the area. Always a spooky proposition when the enemy has a better knowledge than you of the surrounding area. Never a good idea to be in the same place too long. With everyone knowing our location, the chances of mortars raining down becomes a concern.

Our work was done, time to move on.

CHAPTER 41:

Bee-ware

———◆—◆——

FIREBASE: ARTILLERY OUTPOST. COMES IN TWO FLAVORS, one in the rear with the big guns (155s, 175s, 8"); the other in the field (105s and mortars).

Bees. Gotta love 'em.

Visiting the West Coast recently found me hanging out with friends on their 14 acres located on a beautiful island in the Northwest. I asked about the purpose of some box-like structures on the property and was told they were beehives from the previous owner.

I've always had a passing interest in bees and had been following with concern over the past few years the great decline in bee populations. Colony collapse disorder resulted in the loss of 50 percent of North American bee populations in 2006 alone.

They're making a comeback of sorts, but it highlights the fragile balance of life that connects us all.

Bees are a small insect with a big impact on many levels. A food source, plant pollinators, critical to our environment and often taken for granted like so many other species we share the planet with, many on the verge of extinction.

Making my way home from the West Coast found me facing a long layover in Phoenix, Arizona. I took the opportunity to link up with a fellow Trooper from my outfit in the O'Deuce/101st Airborne who lives there. He picked me up at the airport, and we swapped war stories as he showed me the town, stopping to eat some good Mexican food (a must when I'm in that part of the world). Of his many interests, our discussions revealed he was an active beekeeper. He gave me a brief overview of the bee industry and I was able to expand on my bee knowledge. As a bonus, he offered to send me some fresh honey from his hives. Who doesn't love honey? He didn't have to ask twice. It arrived and was long ago consumed, very tasty.

More Bees, Phu Bai, Vietnam

We were separated from the main body of our company. It had moved out to make contact with a large body of NVA troops that had been reported in a nearby village. We stayed back to guard the rucksacks, enabling them to travel lighter with just ammo and water.

It was a small group of us, no more than a half dozen. Largely surrounded by rice paddies, we had taken cover in a tiny bushy area; the village in question was barely visible in the distance. We did have the luxury of an RTO (radio telephone operator) with us to provide a reassuring link should help be needed.

The usual thoughts ran through my mind: best place to take cover if the s*t hits the fan. What if a larger enemy group comes upon us? How to best conserve my ammo in a firefight? And so on.

Then, mortar rounds from our firebase in the distance began landing nearby. This wasn't standard H&I fire (random artillery fire at randomly picked coordinates), but had been called on by the main body of our Troops, now out of sight.

It was instantly obvious to us that the incoming rounds were way off their mark and the firebase had to be notified to make the necessary corrections. Well, we had an RTO with us, he'll just let them know, no problem. But no—there was a big problem.

For security purposes, he was given a new frequency to change to prior to the company setting out, and for whatever reason had forgotten to record the new one.

So, we had mortar rounds dropping nearby, getting closer, no holes to take cover in. The RTO was frantically searching for the new frequency to call off the Incoming. As if that wasn't enough stress, D. disrupts a swarm of bees that were sharing the same group of bushes with us. D. was the only one to get stung. The bee nailed him right between the eyes and immediate swelling of his forehead began. The swelling continued, and D.'s vision was becoming increasingly impaired.

It was like a bad comedy. Mortar rounds exploding, bees swarming, us scrambling to keep away from the bees in a limited space, and at the same time not wanting to run out into the rice paddies, exposing ourselves to potential enemy fire.

Well, none too soon the mystery frequency was located, the Incoming rounds called off, and the bees moved on, to our great relief.

The encounter with the NVA in the village didn't come about. We rejoined the company and everyone had a good laugh at D.'s bee sting. The swelling was pretty severe, but with treatment it subsided.

No, he didn't get a Purple Heart with Bee cluster.

Not the same for the bees. We can only speculate about how many of them and other small species we covered in blankets of Agent Orange. The use of this toxic chemical was not only to the detriment of Vietnam but the world at large, as we are interconnected in ways we've yet to discover.

CHAPTER 42:

Halloween

———◆———

THEY TOOK COVER RIGHT BESIDE ME. AS A STONE WALL it was one of the better places to be. Much better than the small bush my buddy Al Painter sheltered behind, as he described to me in his recounting of the day.

Twenty feet to my front, my squad leader took a direct burst from an AK to the chest. "I'm hit"—his only words. He managed to crawl back, collapsing just behind me. Our medic reached him and began an attempt to save his life. As in all cases of this type, we radioed for a dustoff chopper. Landing, though, will have to wait until if and when we can secure the area.

The weapons fire was coming from my front. We had been making our way through a few farming hooches on the edge of a rice paddy, itself in a valley. The vegetation to my front was much thicker, with little visibility. With my '79 I was in an ideal spot to lob a few rounds over our guys and hopefully with some effect. Thank God the '79 is breech loaded. As a single-shot weapon, I was loading one round at a time. Because of the trembling of my hands, I had difficulty placing the round in the chamber. Another concern was the bulky size of my ammo supply was dwindling fast. This being my first engagement in my first week in the Boonies, lessons had to be soaked up fast. The individual who had taken me under his wing the night before and had been giving me pointers now lay dying. I decided to ease back and make the shots count.

The two old Vietnamese men taking cover with me were every bit as scared as I was, probably more so, with no weapons to defend themselves. They appeared to be farmers. Each dressed the same: shirt, shorts, and sandals. In their 50s or 60s? One of them was blind in one eye. Holding my position, firing occasionally, trying to determine where the fire is coming from. We were all pinned down.

Then I hear the jet support we had called for come screaming in at tree-top level. I briefly glimpsed the F-4 streaking by. A napalm container is released and quietly tumbles end-over-end. The napalm impacts, the ground releasing a huge mushroom cloud of flames, quickly replaced by billowing black smoke that made for a terrifying sight. I'm simultaneously struck by the accuracy of the targeting, the proximity to our position, and the noise of the jets. A couple more passes, this time with 250-pound high-explosive bombs. These weren't quiet. The noise and shock wave it produced was overpowering, competing with my fear of what's up ahead for attention.

Rather than the one platoon patrolling alone, we were two platoons patrolling in strength. Given the heavy NVA activity in the area, a little extra manpower proved critical. The rest of the company remained on a nearby hill top, beyond immediate help.

B. crawled up to my position.

Immediately he put the muzzle of his '16 to the chest of one of the Vietnamese men right on my left. The Vietnamese was now facing me. B. pushed at one and indicated he wanted the man to go over the wall in the direction from which we were receiving fire. Why and for what reason, I can only guess. Terrified, the Vietnamese could not respond. A quick burst and the Vietnamese slumped back into the wall, killed instantly. He remained facing me in a half-sitting position, his eyes half open, lids ever so slowly closing.

The second Vietnamese, same demand. B. once more points his '16 against the man's chest, pushing and shouting at him to get over the wall. More terrified than the first one, the Vietnamese attempts to talk, lips moving weakly. Words fail to come.

Two quick shots, this time on semiautomatic. He too slumps in a position like the other. It doesn't take long, the flies start gathering.

Holy s**t, what? Why? What for ? It's not something I inquired about. I was too concerned with my own survival for the time being. I recall a friend of mine at the head of the column telling me that he felt they were aware of the ambush we were walking into and felt no remorse with their deaths. Farmers caught in the middle? NVA sympathizers, who knows?

Enemy fire begins to die down, reinforcements from our company link up with us. The NVA break off contact, but not before firing off some parting rounds from across the rice paddy. By now they had circled to my right flank. I returned fire. Their fire fades away, they're gone. Not too soon, I've less than a dozen rounds left.

The dustoff chopper descends. My squad leader and other wounded are taken away. Fresh ammo is brought in.

Checking out the area we uncover a wooden chest containing written NVA propaganda. Many paper slips asking why, as GIs, we were in their country, and asking us to leave.

Zippos out, we torch the hooches, kill some pigs and chickens, and we're out of there.

We move on back up the hill to rejoin our company. Trying to come to terms of the day's events and settling my nerves, the respite is short lived. Not again?! A '79 is called for, I'm close by and respond. Looking downhill with his binoculars, F. spots some NVA. It's pretty well the maximum range for my '79. I'm trying to get my bearings by aiming the 50 degrees or so at some cloud while F. adjusts my aim according to the impact of the rounds. An NVA is hit, and then managed to crawl out of sight. Too far for us to verify the results. Fine with me, I've had more than enough for one day.

It's going to be a long year. Boredom at the bank looks good now.

Hey…wait a minute!

The above, only a page or so for what actually took place over a period of eight to nine hours?

The difficulty in putting down events of this type are many. Much of what goes on in a firefight is simultaneous with other events taking place. They don't happen in a sequential way that makes for easy description.

Eyes, ears, smell, touch, even the salty taste of sweat. Every sense in the body kicks in at 1000%.

In war movies, cameras often pan from above or various angles. Slow-motion action is depicted. Our view is often barely a foot above the ground. The rounds cracking overhead at more than twice the speed of sound make sure of that.

The heat and dirt, our bodies pumping out tons of adrenaline, heart beating like crazy, the incoming artillery with the deafening impact of HE rounds. The shudder of the ground from bombs falling. AK rounds flying by, tracers appearing like light swords from Star Wars. The dreaded cracking sounds made by AKs, these I had been warned of before arriving in Vietnam. The intense stress of making sure that as our linking reinforcements got closer, it has to be to the point that we can see them or vice versa and we don't shoot each other.

Residual fires still flickering, caused by the napalm, smell of underbrush still burning. The occasional crack of bamboo air chambers exploding from the fires, mimicking that of an AK round.

The never ending gargling sound of blood from the "sucking chest wound" my squad leader had, another unpleasant event I had been warned of. Each breath long and strained yet never seeming to end.

Placing him on a poncho, used as a stretcher, four of us grabbing a corner and making the dash for the dustoff chopper.

He died the next day at the hospital.

The confusion of the half dozen or so other wounded from RPG, small arms, and other booby traps.

The squeal of a pig that refused to go quietly as it was repeatedly bayoneted.

The fact that there were fewer of us now than when the day began.

Halloween is around the corner as I write this—those events took place in October, 1967.

The day I recounted was like being in a House of Horrors: You get the s**t scared out of you, and then on to the next room...

Now the silence screams by its contrast to all that went before. Cautiously making our way forward, the monsters are now real. We just don't know when they will jump out at us, not with a "Boo" but with any/every device that can be used to shred us. All illusions are gone, games are over, reality is here big time!

CHAPTER 43:

Headache

—◆—

I VIEWED MY BODY IN THREE PARTS AT THE TIME. MY head, which was on fire with a pounding headache. Everything below my neck felt chilled and trembling. Then there was my left elbow, swollen to the size of a football and immovable. My temperature was hovering in the 104-degree range and not going down.

The medics had me on a cot at the battalion aid station. Stripped naked they placed ice packs under each of my armpits and between my legs by my groin.

The chills kept prompting me to reach for a sheet to cover myself and the medics kept taking it from me.

That morning had seen me wake up with a headache and slightly sore elbow.

I looked to see if I had been bitten by one of the many usual suspects (snakes, scorpion, spiders, etc.). Nothing definitive.

In no time my condition escalated. Headache getting really bad, fever, same, elbow stiffening and getting more swollen.

The medic decided I needed urgent care and I was to be sent to the rear area to be attended to. A dustoff medivac chopper was to be called. Seeing that we were not too far from our firebase, the question was posed to me if I felt well enough to hump my way over to the firebase and "hitchhike" my way to the rear on one of the many choppers still coming and going from that location.

In one of those decisions that I came to regret, my response was "Sure Sarge, I can do that." The fever must have fried my brain to have agreed to such a brain-dead idea.

Lighting up my rucksack, I removed my C-rations and LRRPs and gave them to my buddies. Then off I went.

Though not that far from the firebase, I was, after all, alone and there were Charlies in the area. Overcoming that concern, I finally stumbled into the firebase, and explain my predicament to the powers that be. Sit tight, I'm told, we'll have a chopper for you soon.

Sit tight I did. I could almost touch the 105s that were firing away beside me. Boom went my headache, Boom answered the 105, BOOM went my head. Back and forth, my head and the 105s had a kettle drum solo going on.

Finally, here's my chopper. The thudding, whooping sounds of the blades do not help my headache one bit.

Nooooo! The FO (forward observer) decided to commandeer my chopper to go spot for the artillery against NVA that have been seen in the valley.

Over an hour passed, before they got me to the rear at the Battalion aid station mentioned above.

From there they decided to bump me up to the 22nd surgical hospital on the other side of the base.

And yes, the bumps were plenty on the Jeep ride to the hospital. Every little pothole made my head ring. I was about to tell them to just let me off and die by the side of the road, because my head couldn't take any more pounding.

Finally, they dropped me off at the ER. Sitting in the waiting room, I'm reading signs to past the time. NO ORDINANCE allowed. WEAPONS NO! EXPLOSIVES not permitted. Check your WEAPONS at the door. From a killing zone to a healing zone.

Almost there, but one final delay. Straight out of a M.A.S.H. scene, dustoff choppers come swooping in, stretchers and bodies tied to IV's race by me on their way to the operating rooms. I'm too preoccupied with my own pain to care.

Amen, a doctor came, and they immediately started me on antibiotics. Penicillin, tetracycline, and another one which I can't recall at the moment. As a target area to insert these injections my butt was chosen. Three at a time, multiple times a day. The nurse would come, flip me over, left cheek, right cheek. After a while I lost track of which cheek was up next, take your pick I'd tell her.

My fever still remained high. The dreaded ice bath was now being contemplated. That's right, soaking in a big slurpy of crushed ice. I've heard about these treatments which were used for malaria, not a fun thought.

Or, the doctor said I could go and stand under the shower and see if that will lower my fever. A no brainer: The shower it was.

Feeling the water run over my body for a good while. I felt the fever subside ever so slightly. The tide was turning.

Over the next week or so saw the swelling lessen to where I could flex my arm. Headache went away, I was healing, yeah!!

The hospital was like a five-star hotel compared to the Boonies. Still, it's not like the Army to let manpower go to waste. So while still in the hospital, they volunteered me for some light duty. I had a choice of filling sandbags to be used in fortifications or bunkers, or helping to feed some wounded soldiers unable to feed themselves.

Well, spoons are lighter than sandbags and out of the heat, so I chose the second. It was. It was rewarding duty and I was able to swap stories with GIs from different units. One guy I fed was wrapped up like a mummy. Others were in various stages of recovery. The worse cases were in the ICU, many with injuries too horrible to contemplate.

My hospital room consisted of many beds shared with other recovering soldiers.

At one point some officers came through to distribute Purple Hearts to the wounded. One GI was there being treated for syphilis; an awkward moment ensued (I don't think Patton would have approved). Another had a sexy scar on his face, grazed by a round from a 45, but from an encounter with a hooker that had gone bad.

Malaria, tendonitis? The doctors would never know for sure what was the true cause of my illness. But, I was better and gung ho to rejoin my outfit and see my buddies.

Back at the battalion rear area, I'm there to greet my unit as they returned from the Boonies.

My first impression in seeing them was how incredibly dirty/scruffy they looked, and boy, did they ever STINK!

To my friend A.: Did I miss anything? Not much: He did regret cutting the ear off a dead Charlie. He had been shot through the head with a '16.

He described his head as bag of crushed ice. Yep, a '16 will definitely do that to you. I was back into that dimension where crazy and insane is to be rewarded.

CHAPTER 44:

Christmas Day

---

50 YEARS TO THE MONTH ON WHICH THESE EVENTS took place.

I turned the bits of shattered metal between my thumb and forefingers. Then I made the connection.

The day had been progressing well.

Our company was feeling more festive than usual, our location high in the Central Highlands near Bao Loc.

The terrain was more rugged and steep than what we normally encountered, but for the time being our thoughts were elsewhere.

It was Christmas Day, and we were being resupplied with choppers coming and going. We had made little contact with any enemy for the past couple of weeks and everyone was feeling at ease, for the most part. Also, being in what was thought to be a fairly secure location resulted in a brown-bag meal brought out to us, supplementing our boring Cs.

Two more surprises were added to the mix in the form of USO girls making the trip out on this resupply. They aided in handing out our mail and packages normally held in the rear area awaiting our return from the Boonies. Having the packages from home, containing much-desired Christmas goodies, was a bonus that was the icing on the cake. Some Troopers had multiple packages and shared their good fortune with the rest of us.

I received one package, compliments of the American Legion, the only one I was to get while in Vietnam. It came about due to putting my name in a jar when I was Stateside getting a final haircut before shipping out to 'Nam.

It could not have been more welcome. It contained a tin of cookies and other incidentals. What I didn't devour was squeezed into the top of my rucksack, itself already maxed out with a fresh supply of Cs and ammo. Life was good, zero complaints.

In our squad area we had selected a tree that somewhat resembled a Christmas tree and decorated it with Christmas cards, candy canes, and shaving cream to simulate snow. Though somewhat scraggly, and nothing near the sculptured Christmas trees found in many homes, to us it looked better than the Christmas tree at Rockefeller Center in New York. Pictures were taken, smiles all around.

The choppers had now left and the swirl of activity had quieted down. It wasn't long before we would move out to resume our routine of patrols in search of the enemy. For now though, I was savoring the good vibes of the day as I lugged my rucksack to the perimeter, where I prepared to take my turn on guard.

I laid my weapon against a log, careful to keep it out of any dirt, and positioned my rucksack close to it with its tin of cookies peeking out at me, making me smile.

I plopped myself on the ground, pivoting my back to secure the rucksack as a backrest, searching for the most comfortable position, trying to avoid straps and buckles digging into my back and stones from the ground digging into my butt. It was at this moment I heard a slight rustle directly in front of me.

Raising my gaze, I was met with the stare of a Vietnamese male looking directly at me. Neither of us moved a muscle.

He had stopped his progress through thick bushes no more than 20 feet in front of me. I froze, bringing a halt to my search for seating comfort. Between us, a slight clearing.

All I could see of him was his head, with no hat or helmet that would aid me in determining his identity. Red scarf around his neck, everything below that blocked by dense undergrowth. He looked young, his face blank of expression.

I didn't feel fear, but more a sense of irritation at what I thought could only be one of the interpreters who traveled with our company. It flashed through my mind that he had gone out beyond our perimeter to relieve himself and returned to the wrong location. Who else could it be? All the commotion of the recent resupply would have deterred any activity at this point.

Still, it didn't add up, and our gazes remained locked, no movement or expression on his part or mine. Gears whirled in my head searching for an answer to the mystery before me. Just to be on the safe side, having my weapon in my hands would be a good bet.

The trouble was that my '79 was just out of reach by about a foot.

This was further complicated by the fact that a '79 is a single-shot weapon and the HE round I had in its breech wasn't the best for this scenario. Still, something is better than nothing.

I break my gaze and reach for the '79 as casually as I can. The following fraction of time was shattered by a loud burst of automatic-weapons fire. I instantly scrambled for cover. Any doubt as to the identity of my mystery intruder was cleared. NVA.

I must have rocketed 50 feet before realizing that miraculously I had not been hit and to my amazement, no further weapons fire followed to cut me down. This was contrary to past experience where all hell usually breaks loose following an initial burst.

Not here, just one burst and the NVA took off.

Another miracle: My '79 was still by my rucksack.

This was similar to when I was at a party and accidentally placed my palm on a hot stove, yanking it back without thought. So too was my shock and reaction to obtain cover once the sound of the burst hit my ears.

This left me exposed and sheepish among a group of GIs looking at me with questioning looks.

Regrouping, frags were thrown in the direction I indicated the NVA Trooper to be. No return of fire? He'd booked out.

Initially, I hadn't believed that he was as close to me as indicated. Then spent 9-mm casings were found at the location I pointed out, confirming my story. Nine-mm rounds were not the AK-47 rounds we expected and not that common. Normally they went with 9-mm automatic pistols issued to NVA officers.

It turned out I was the only one to have seen him. The other perimeter guards to my immediate flanks were unaware of the NVA's presence the whole time everything transpired.

The fallout began.

My reputation as a fighter had up to this point held its own, but was now rapidly falling under retelling. They mistakenly said that I had just up and run when I had no chance to explain in detail the context of what transpired.

So how could he have missed, given the very small distance between us?

Later that evening, in a new night location, I was preparing my coffee and dug through a pouch on the side of my rucksack. I noticed a clean hole through a bundle of instant Kool Aid and hot chocolate packs kept together with a rubber band. It dawned on me what I was looking at as I inspected the shattered metal end of my trip flare. It was destroyed by a round that would have penetrated my chest had I not moved a microsecond sooner.

I turned the bits of shattered round between my thumb and forefingers, bits and pieces of it.

I took those bits and pieces and wrapped them up in a Chiclets gum package, intending to take it home with me, only to accidentally toss it out at a later time.

What happened to the NVA? Very unusual was the fact that he appeared to be traveling alone. Why did he not follow up with a second burst at me? How come no headgear? What was the reason for his hesitation? Surely there was no mistaking me as anything but a GI.

I don't know if it would have changed anything, but had he worn the standard NVA helmet, it would have tipped me off to his identity and not caused me to hesitate.

The same day this event took place, far below in the valley, our company recon outfit was patrolling. Alerted to what happened, they set an ambush and killed a lone NVA. His weapon was a 9-mm automatic pistol.

CHAPTER 45:

Recruiting Office

———————◆———————

WITH MY MIND MADE UP, I FOUND MYSELF IN THE
recruiting office and ready to implement my plan. Typical of all recruiting offices the pictures on the walls are gung-ho, positive, and patriotic.
Invincible and overwhelming military might projecting victory everywhere. No gross dead bodies on display, limbs missing, voices of the suffering in one's head. Go to a VA Hospital if that's what you want to see.

Flags, tanks, ships, jets, all designed to project the might of military
at its best. The recruiters— veterans themselves with multiple ribbons on
their chest—were there to reassure and most of all to RECRUIT.

To remind everyone, I had a (double) draft deferment and could have
avoided this whole scenario. My decision to take this step was to secure the
GI Bill to pay the four years of college, and I was hoping to secure work
within the army that could expand my skills there. Yes, the war in Vietnam
was ratcheting up to its peak, and experiencing the whole affair from the
sidelines had a certain appeal. Additionally, my present employer was obli-
gated to allow me to return to my job upon leaving the service, should I
choose. It looked like a win-win.

The fact that I was not a U.S. citizen at the time but a Canadian with a
Green Card did not faze the recruiters in the least. (It did, however, greatly
affect later events, so pay attention.)

So, what branch of service to enlist in and in what capacity?

The Air Force was my first choice; hey, I love all things that fly. But the minimum four-year requirement represented about 21% of my life at my age then, 19. A hell of a long time, I thought. Oh how time flies now. Four years now seems like a piece of cake.

As for the Navy, it was the same thing, four years. Plus I could be stuck sailing the oceans for months at a time. Nope!

Marines? Are you crazy? A person could get killed.

The Army had a three-year enlistment term as opposed to the two years required for draftees. Less than 16% of my 19 years. I could live with that. Now, what to select for my MOS (Military Occupation Specialty)—my job description?

As an enlistee I was allowed an MOS of my choice. This is an inducement for those who enlist. Get drafted and it's pot luck, or out of luck, and off to the Infantry.

I wanted something related to my current work in computers, but nothing like that was available. As an alternative, they offered me a job working with cryptographic machines. Hmmm, spy stuff, not bad. James Bonds movies were coming out strong and hitting the big screen, drawing record crowds. Sounds cool, sounds safe. I pictured working with Army Intelligence in the DC area, not bad. That'll work. Where do I sign?

So began my three-year stint in Uncle Sam's Army, in the year 1966.

My Mom wasn't aware of the decision until after the fact. In hindsight, I'm sure she wouldn't have been thrilled had I told her beforehand. My parents split right after my high school graduation in a nasty divorce and she counted on my presence more than I realized.

She had been brought up in the World War II generation and viewed any war with more realistic eyes. No doubt with a heavy heart, she saw me off from the train station in Fort Wayne, Detroit (a real Fort, not to be confused with Fort Wayne, Indiana) loaded with other new recruits on our way to Fort Knox, Kentucky. The initial step on my military adventures.

I would be one new recruit added to the 500,000-plus servicemen serving in Vietnam when I arrived there. Later, in the course of writing this book, just for the heck of it, I jumped on my motorcycle and went down to visit Fort Wayne, in Detroit, a mere 25 miles from where I presently live.

Located in an old industrial section of Detroit on the Detroit River, I found it in a sad state.

Technically an historic site, its less than desirable location and little upkeep presented a depressing scene. Pulling up to the guard gate, after avoiding numerous potholes, the guard points me to the check-in building.

Of the many buildings that comprise the original Fort Wayne, many are literally falling apart.

I pull up to the best of the worst and locate someone, also a Vietnam vet, who gives me brief tour and overview. Despite it being in serious need of funding and restoration, there were facts and history to appreciate about the site. There is also a small museum dedicated to the Tuskegee Airmen. I missed out on their tour as it was by appointment only. Next time.

I pulled away, carefully dodging those same potholes, bad roads, trucking warehouses, and construction detours, while passing countless boarded-up houses, and headed home.

Maybe another time, I thought. And, hey! It was a nice day for a ride.

CHAPTER 46:

Medals/Awards

———◆—◆———

EACH MEDAL PINNED ON A UNIFORM IS IN ITSELF A LIT-
tle storybook. Identical medals often do not tell the same story. Some are
generic and differ little in what they indicate. There are those that indicate
service in various theaters of operation—Vietnam, Korea, Iraq, etc. These
require little explanation other than the dates of service in those various
parts of the world.

Prized among Army Infantrymen is the Combat Infantryman Badge
(CIB). It's only given to Army personnel who have an Infantry MOS and
have come under fire in a combat setting. It looks like a rifle with a wreath
around it. Normally it sits on top of your stack of other medals.

Jump Wings are another easily identifiable award. They are a silver
medal, a parachute with wings on each side, given to Paratroopers. Some
have stars on them to show an increased level of proficiency.

Purple Hearts, awarded for those wounded in combat, is another
commonly identified medal. Open their story books and the stories are
vast and differing in scope and severity.

Though many rounds came near, by, around, and over, and have hit
my rucksack, luckily I've never been wounded. Aside from bruises and
scratches from exploding bunkers, they were never severe enough to take
me out of the fight.

Pain and discomfort are needed to wear a Purple Heart on your chest. The wounds range from the obviously visible (missing limbs, scars, eyesight); to the invisible (missing internal organs, PTSD, recurring diseases, chemical exposure); to the completely invisible (those spending the remainder of their lives in a vegetative state in VA Hospitals and nursing homes).

Then there are awards for bravery. In the order from lowest to highest, these are the Bronze Star with V (for "valor"), the Silver Star, the Distinguished Service Cross, and the Medal of Honor.

If there is a star on top of these awards, that represents more than one award of the same type.

Again, behind each of these medals is a story that might take up a whole book.

It's important to note that for each medal or award, a set orders is issued that validates/confirms the authenticity of the recipient. These orders are made then part of their military records/archives. I mention this because we all know in this day and age of online purchases, any number of people can (and do) purchase ribbons/medals, real or bogus. Then these sad wannabes try to pass themselves off as legit.

Time passed and retirement arrives. What to do with those medals/awards? Well, many of us put them in a display case to be displayed in our homes. Display case, a shrine of sorts—in any event, it's not a bad idea to show those who are interested that there was a time in our lives that we were part of something epic. Sadly the display case, some of the best deserve, never makes it past the point of a tombstone or their name on a memorial wall.

Third Platoon, Charlie Company, 2/502, First Brigade, 101st Airborne Division, of which I was part, was in continuous combat roles from the mid-1960s to the early 1970s, and earned enough medals to fill a five-gallon bucket.

Our 3rd Platoon, in Charlie Co., 2/502 alone has seen two of our Troopers awarded the DSC (Distinguished Service Cross for Valor), which is the second-highest award for valor possible, while I was there. I fought alongside both of them. One had been my platoon sergeant, and another my squad leader at one point.

Woe be to them who find themselves discussing their bogus feats with real Vets, those who can spot the inconsistencies and lies.

Looking back, I sometimes wish I had a bigger collection of medals to show for my time there.

But all those medals come at a price. The price can far exceed anything that they can display to compensate for the medal awarded. I've learned over my life to be careful about what you wish for.

However, I'm going to award myself the Combat Author's medal. I don't think there is such a critter. Just the same, it'll do the job for me. Too big to pin on my chest: It's this book. Which gives an overview of what goes on in war, variations of which sadly continue to this day.

CHAPTER 47:

Tornado

———◆———

Joplin, Missouri, May 22, 2011

EARLIER THAT DAY SAW ME DOING MY USUAL ROUTINE, taking the shuttle bus to Wal-Mart, and then getting some much needed exercise by walking to the Starbucks at the mall a mile away and back again. Always a pleasant change from trucks, truck stops, and the surrounding noise. As I prepared most of my meals in the truck, a welcome meal at a restaurant didn't hurt.

My T-2000 Kenworth Tractor with its N-14 Big Cam Cummins Motor was in the shop undergoing regular preventative maintenance (PM). Both that engine and cab style are no longer made, having been replaced with a newer, more fuel-efficient engine. The cab retained its practical aerodynamic design and its roomy standup sleeper that made for a cozy inn through the years. Best of all, it was paid for.

The PM should be done by the time I do my thing. Then hook up to the trailer and back on the road to knock off the remaining 800 miles to Detroit for my time off. Once in Detroit, I'll relay the trailer to continue on its destination to Toronto, Canada.

I had picked up the load at our Laredo, Texas terminal. Then up I-35, through San Antonio, Austin, Waco, Dallas, head due north, pick up Highway 75 to Sherman, Texas into Oklahoma. Jump on Highway 69, and continue through Durant, McAlester, Muskogee, and Big Cabin, where I jump on I-44 and cut east for Joplin, Missouri, the location of our main terminal.

All of the above located smack in the middle of Tornado Alley. During my 20 years as a trucker with this truckload company, and coming up on 2 million miles (all with the same company), I had witnessed some tornadoes and driven through the results of many more. The chaotic and erratic trail of destruction they left never ceased to amaze me.

I had intended to make it to the mall, but stopped to grab a bite to eat at my favorite local Thai restaurant. While eating I glanced up at the weather channel and tracked the fast moving storm cells. My guess was that they might miss us, as they looked to be tracking a bit to the west. I made a decision to curtail my walk and head back to the terminal. I was almost back at Wal-Mart to pick up the shuttle bus when the tornado sirens began kicking in, with their long wails.

It was getting seriously dark.

Linking up with the shuttle van, our driver went to check on the whereabouts of one last individual. He finds that Wal-Mart had locked the doors and not permitted anyone to leave, directing customers inside to designated tornado shelters. The tornado sirens have intensified and their wails are now continuous.

We're out of here! Pedal to the metal for our clunker shuttle van and back to the terminal.

At the shop, my truck is outside the shop and ready to go, the PM completed.

I'm ready to go but will the weather let me? Finishing up the required paperwork, I look out the door.

A massive wall of black sky is heading our way. I ask the mechanic where the tornado shelter is. The mechanic points to the slit trench in the shop floor. Somewhat stunned, I ask, "That's it?" All this time I'd assumed this building had an underground tornado shelter, as did our main building a quarter mile away. No time to make the dash there. I jump in, thinking, this is a real sketchy setup. Believing I'm alone in the trench, I hear a voice calling, "We have room here." Tucked off to the side of the trench is a recessed area for oil and grease hoses coiled on their spools. The two mechanics make space and I shoehorn myself in and hook my arm through one of the spoked spools and hang on.

The wind builds to a roar with the day darkening at the same time. Ping, ping, ping, ping, ping, the rollers on the 700-pound steel rollup doors are ripped from their spring tracks and are sent flying. The doors bang and crash inwards on the floor, the roof is ripped, sides of the building, are torn away.

Through the whole thing I felt as exposed as that cartoon frog clinging to the side of a whirling blender doing its best not to fall in. How flying sheet metal, oil drums, tool chests, and tires avoided dropping on us and slicing us up was nothing short of a miracle. A few minor injuries, but we all made it out OK.

Walking outside to survey the damage I saw 53-foot trailers weighing up to 60,000 pounds that had been tossed around. Many knocked over like dominos where they sat parked in what had been neat rows. Some 20,000-pound tractors had been picked up and dropped on the other side of the shop. Trees, debris, sheet metal, and insulation were everywhere. Looking east at the Flying J truck stop, more destruction. The Wal-Mart I was at just before, was totaled; the Home Depot beside it, leveled.

The elation of survival was soon displaced with a shudder of fear I hadn't felt in years. Where? In Vietnam 43 years earlier, toward the later part of my tour. The firefight over, brief elation at having come out on top, bodies and destruction around me. Then, a clinging fog of darkness I could no longer shake that grew as the weeks followed.

The time had come to reconsider my options. Gone are the days when I'd drive into storms, high winds, hail, and sheets of rain and snow, knowing I'd somehow punch through the other side.

My body was OK but my confidence had been sucked from me that day, by that tornado.

My truck suffered a bit of damage, with a side fairing torn away.

My trailer was still in the ready line waiting for me, untouched.

If I can pick my way through the debris, I'm getting out of here. Which is just what I did.

I later found out that over 160 people died in Joplin that day, and many more were seriously injured. In terms of money it was the most destructive tornado ever in the United States.

A few months later, again passing through Joplin, the head mechanic pulled me aside, one of those who had been in the trench with me. He wanted me to look at footage from one of our security cameras that was pointed right at my tractor less than 15 feet away during the tornado. It showed the mounting rain and wind, just about obscuring the truck at one point. Then the side fairing being ripped off and the gradual subsiding of the wind.

An easy cosmetic fix, better that those tractors that had been picked up and dropped a hundred yards away.

Above

I took shelter in the truck maintenance building pictured here. That is my truck just outside the door with some damage on the air fairing. On the building itself doors and roof were torn off. I took shelter in the "grease pit", the narrow-lit area seen on the shop floor.

Above

Many of our trailers ended up like this.

The weight of these trailer can range from~20,000-60,000 lb.

Luckily mine awaited me undamaged and I
hooked to it and continued onto Detroit.

Above
Back in Detroit, my Truck patched up and painted
after surviving the Joplin tornado.

Below

Just shy of logging 2,000,000 miles before my retirement From CFI/Conway Trucking.

Shown below are my various safety patches and my 1,000,000 mile Commemorative Plaque.

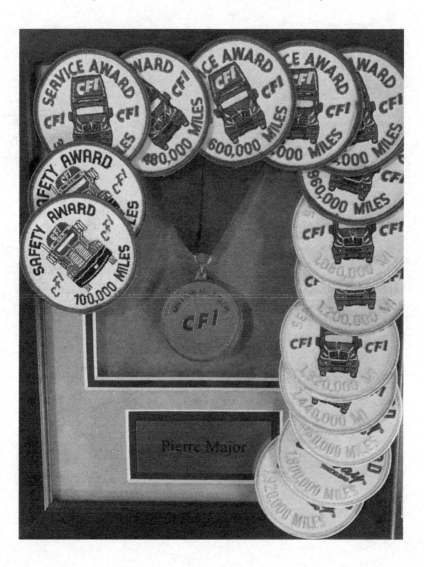

CHAPTER 48:

Trip Flare

DAMNIT! I ACCIDENTALLY TRIGGERED MY TRIP FLARE! We placed them just beyond our perimeter to illuminate NVA that might be sneaking up on us.

Generally set every evening at dusk and always a dicey situation at best, they were super easy to set off and once triggered, impossible to extinguish.

Yes, the vegetation is thick, but that's usually the case. I had tied off my trip flare to a small tree, successfully stringing the wire, and was gingerly backing off to the perimeter when POP! I had hit a twig, which pulled a vine, that yanked another twig and knocked off a few ants, which landed on the trip wire and game over.

Magnesium was burning white-hot, emitting an intense light for the whole world to see. Impossible to extinguish unless you could smother it with mud.

I did the next best thing. I whipped off my helmet and removed the helmet liner in one motion. Then dropped the steel pot onto the trip flare to cover the light. Now it was a waiting game while it burned itself out. In the meantime, I watched my camouflage cover on the steel pot get fried to a crisp.

The pot turned a glowing red in the process.

The flare finally extinguished, I return the now black-and-burnt steel pot to my liner. My next camouflage cover will be leaving me with bad vibes.

A cherry mistake indeed. The standard punishment awaits me once we get to the rear on stand down: digging a 3 foot by 3 foot by 3 foot hole with an entrenching tool. The hole of shame!

A cubic yard of dirt, which doesn't sound like a lot, but with the sun beating down on you while everyone else is partying and kicking back, it was not fun.

Worse: Everybody and his dog knows our location now. Preventable or not, it's the type of accident that can cost lives by revealing our location to the enemy.

Helmet Liner (about a month later)

I hear the radio crackling in the background, with desperate, frantic voices coming through mixed with sounds of automatic weapons fire. The same automatic weapons fire I'm hearing in the distance. Like lightning in the distance to be followed by the clap of thunder, there's a similar pause.

One of our squads on patrol ran into an ambush.

Leaving rucksacks behind, taking only ammo and our LBE, we go off to help.

Now, think about it. No address, no trails or markings to guide us. Only a general direction and the volume of weapons fire to mark a bearing. Though we would like to get there ASAP, the erratic terrain plus not knowing if the NVA is between us and those we want to link up with, or the other way around, makes us tread carefully. The closer we get, the greater our fear of friendly-fire casualties. With similar color uniforms as that of the NVA, one has to be careful not to shoot at random. It takes us the better part of an hour to reach our guys. With us now having the superior firepower, the NVA break off.

B. in the ambushed squad is dead, and two or three are wounded. W. broke his wrist diving for cover. B. was hit with small arms fire and caught shrapnel from a frag he was throwing at the same moment.

We call choppers to take away the dead and wounded. Top off with more ammo and it's back to business, more patrols, to hump those Boonies, and more patrols.

Now I'm not a superstitious person by nature, but I wasn't thrilled when someone tossed me the camouflage cover from B.'s helmet and I was ordered to put it on my charred steel pot, still black from the trip flare incident.

As I stretch it over my blackened helmet, I notice many little holes and tears in the camouflage material made by the exploding frag the instant B. was shot. Now I'm wearing a dead man's camouflage cover? Bad juju.

I won't be able to get rid of this fast enough and swap it out for a new one once I get to the rear.

CHAPTER 49:

Brian

———◆———

I INTEND TO VISIT HIM TODAY AT HIS NURSING HOME..
Of us four brothers, me being the oldest, he's just below me in age.

They charge 5-star prices, but I often find the service and ambiance to reflect more like 2.5 stars. If it wasn't for the additional help I arranged for him, I would drop that to 1.5 stars.

That said, it's infinitely better than what serves as a nursing home for many of the mentally ill: Jail.

The nursing home he lives in makes for a 50-mile round trip. Taking the backroads on my motorcycle has made that aspect of visiting him more fun and less costly than in my pickup.

His past five or six years there, plus a couple of close calls with bouts of pneumonia that almost cost him his life, have opened my eyes to more of the workings of the VA system than I cared for. I'm on a first-name basis with nurses, doctors, social workers, and staff, both at the nursing home and the nearby VA Hospital.

There's the good and the bad. Some of the staff go above and beyond. Some just punch a clock. Staffing shortages are an ongoing issue.

Blind, non-ambulatory, incontinent for the most part, he's a bit of a mess, with a 100% disability rating.

Schizophrenia is the illness that began his decline.

In hindsight, I could see the symptoms in his early teens, the classic age at which they normally appear. His first psychotic breakdown was in the late 1960s, but not the last. Luckily (if it can be called that), the schizophrenia manifested itself in his final year in the army, allowing access to medical care.

If not for that, there is no doubt in my mind he would be homeless, on the streets, in jail, or... dead—the fate of many seriously mentally ill in his predicament.

I lived thousands of miles from him at the time his initial psychotic episode took place, and had enough on my plate with my own issues. I was already out of the Army when word of his status reached me through my sister.

Just the same, as long as his medications are working properly, and his delusions are in check, there are goals he enjoys striving for. In his mind he's convinced he's taking undergraduate courses at various colleges. He loves learning, even as his health is rapidly fading. To that end I do what I can to provide him with books on tape.

His world view stopped at about the time he lost his sight. He knows about computers and only in a vague, general sense. The concepts and capabilities of what computers can do are beyond him. As an indication of where his timeline is with technology, let me say that he feels an almost obsession to use and own a typewriter. This continues even though he can barely put two letters together given his failing health. I've bought him numerous typewriters over the years, which he has dropped, broken, and generally messed up despite the best efforts of myself or the staff to maintain them. As I type away writing this book on my computer keyboard, I'm struck how these QUERTY keys have intertwined our lives.

I took up typing in high school to help me in writing essays when typewriters (I'm talking manual keyboards, not the fancy IBM Selectric) were the only game in town when it came to keyboards. The class was almost all girls; that part didn't hurt, but it was a Catholic school and I was a good boy in those days. Darn.

At the time if you looked hard and knew where to look, you might find a computer keyboard. Big, clunky, it would be attached to a mainframe computer, and only one.

Eventually my typing skills led to an Army MOS as an IBM keypuncher (even more clunky keyboards but with the same QUERTY layout), and back to this book.

Computer keyboards would be the better option, but his lack of dexterity and inability to grasp computer concepts in general make the idea a non-starter.

Tom Hanks, of movie star fame, recently came out with a book called *Uncommon Type*. It turns out that Tom Hanks has this passion for old typewriters and collects them. Who knew? I bought Brian the audio book version of Tom's book, and he likes it. Whatever makes him happy!

Never a religious person as a kid, now he's obsessed with his faith and salvation. He's ready to bend your ear at any time when it comes to theology. We talk about world events, history, and topics he enjoys. It's all about God or the devil at times.

And if his meds are off or for any of a myriad of reasons, it's time to back off; you could see his anger and frustrations build and his paranoia will kick in. You've just become the devil and there is no amount of reason that will convince him otherwise. He's still not beyond taking a swing at the staff or nurses.

All things considered, though, he's a lot more stabilized.

One more item: Patients are allowed two daily smoke breaks outside. Two cigarettes per smoke break maximum.

You can't get him to quit, his COPD notwithstanding. Not that we haven't tried. But he'll declare the start of World War III, hold a sit-down strike, threaten suicide, start cussing out the nurses.

Yes, he can be very, very stubborn.

Brian in the Mid-1950s, Going Back in Time

Two years my junior, I was around 10 and he was 8. He was a sweet kid, and looked like an angel when sleeping.

He always wanted to hang out with me. "Go play with friends your own age," I would say.

Still we did play many games together. Along with my other, next-youngest brother, we'd go to the community swimming pool and hang out all day, play board games, ride our bikes.

Nothing out of the ordinary, except for a couple of things: he would rock himself to sleep, something we'd always try to get him to stop, without luck.

And he could be very, very stubborn.

Brian, Early 1960s

It's about this time schizophrenia will manifest itself, in the early teens. We knew something was out of place. Little was known about mental illness then, and with some of the therapy the cure was worse than the disease. Then, as now, mental illness remains the poor stepchild of the medical community. Funding is short or non-existent. In addition, a huge stigma exists in even admitting it, both for the individual and the family. In some countries and cultures it's taboo for an individual to even have mental illness.

That said...with my hands by my side and not expecting it, WHAM!! In the midst of an argument he punched me hard in the nose. It was totally unexpected and not only that, completely against our unwritten rules of not punching one another in the face or below the belt! Whatever happened to the Geneva Convention?

I was infuriated, and if my mom hadn't gotten between us, he would have been the worse for it. It was about this time in his life where he could display extreme stubbornness that no amount of reason could overcome. At a time when we needed to pull together, he and my next youngest brother decided to go the other way: Staying out late, partying, getting into trouble with the cops.

Damn! That's the second broken bone he gave me. The broken finger that I acquired when we were playing football was excusable. My nose, however, was never the same, with my breathing and sense of smell considerably lessened. We parted ways. I could no longer attempt to insert reason, because he wouldn't listen.

Brian, 1967

December 1967, he arrived in Vietnam with the remainder of the 101st Airborne Division.

The initial contingent of the 101st (the First Brigade) had already been there for a while. I was part of that initial group.

At the time of his arrival I had already been "in-country" for three months. My outfit was operating in a different part of the Vietnam and I wasn't to see him until just before leaving Vietnam.

Headquarters Company contacted me to let me know of his arrival and that he worked in communications as a radio operator at the battalion level. At least his job kept him in the rear area working radios in a heavily fortified bunker.

I had been unaware of his enlistment, not to mention him being in the same division and now the same war zone?! How did that come about? How did he get that "jam" MOS of his?

Headquarters also went on to inform me I had the option of leaving my unit and being reassigned out of Vietnam. Already bonded in combat with my buddies, that didn't feel right. I opted to hang in there a stick out the remaining nine months of my tour. But that was about to change.

Me, March/April 1967

Four months remained in my tour.

It was a mixture of events. These included the area we were in, pushing towards the A Shau valley; my broken eyeglass lens, never fixed despite numerous promises; the seemingly nonstop combat; the alienation and perception or fact of feeling shunned due to the Christmas incident. The constant fears that came and went now came and stayed. It was like being in a fog that never lifted.

So I got out pen and paper and without telling anyone in my platoon, I wrote Brian a letter telling him I was ready to get the hell out of the Boonies and to get in touch with the powers that be and let them know as much.

In other words, I was ready to cash in on the offer they had presented to me four months previously.

Above
Flag and shell casings presented to me by the Honor Guard at my brother Brian's funeral. He died shortly before I completed the Version II of this book.

CHAPTER 50:

Triggers/PTSD

---◆---

02:30-03:00. I OFTEN WAKE TO THE SOUND OF THREE clocks, one of which is a high-pitched "ringing" in my ears due to hearing loss. It's an annoyance during the day and is often masked by the ambient activity of the day, so I can often shrug it off.

In the quiet of the night, however, it's the dominant clock (yes, 12 kHz is a time cycle), driving me nuts. It's like a couple of loud mosquitoes, one in each ear!

The second clock is the regular thumping beat of my heart. A steady, or maybe not too steady, rhythm of 70 beats per minute.

The third clock is the slow, steady inhalations of my breathing. This, to my advantage, I've managed to regulate and gain control of through the practice of Yoga, which places a premium on the control of the breath.

A couple other clocks can also intervene at this time. The quarter-hourly chimes of the grandfather clock from the living room, which also counts off the hours at the top of the hour. The other is a nightstand clock, projecting the time on the ceiling.

I try to ignore them all and fall back asleep. Fifteen minutes can stretch to 30 minutes then to an hour or more.

A sleep clinic I attended at the VA suggests that if you're awake for more than 15 minutes, it's best to get up and do something. Then once your mind has quieted down, you can return to bed.

And that is what I've been doing with moderate success. Since I'm awake, why not see if I can be productive with my time and write about experiences of my time in Vietnam?

The different narratives added up to where I am now.

Triggers, 1970s

I was coming off my night shift as a taxi driver, with the morning light just breaking. It was a weekend gig and I enjoyed it as a second job. Something I liked doing for those two days but that was about it.

I parked my cab and headed for the coffee shop to tally the night's take and shoot the breeze with my fellow cabbies. The coffee shop was situated under a large bridge.

Before entering the coffee shop, not a hundred yards away at the far end of the parking lot, I saw a body crumpled on the asphalt and positioned in a way that I knew said death.

I didn't need to, or care to, get closer to see what happened. I guessed what had happened and was subsequently proved correct.

I knew with that with the comings and goings of our shift change he would be found soon enough, and so he was. A suicide, he jumped from the bridge. An all-too-frequent occurrence from that particular bridge. The bridges in that city included some that were works of art in their own right. I crossed them all in different manners: jogging, walking, biking, driving. It's a pity that rather than using them for their intended purpose—crossing from one side to the other—they are also used to cross from life to death. Often with no answer to the many questions raised by their final action.

In talking to a boat operator who pilots a water taxi under that same bridge, he mentioned to me that the sound of a sudden loud splash nearby would signify a suicide hitting the water. *Bummer*, I thought, such a beautiful spot.

It always bothered me when hearing the word "trigger" associated with the four letters "PTSD." It implied a point of no return, and for a long time that's how it was with me: The trigger went off and a flood of feelings took over that I couldn't counter. And they were right. Once that trigger went off, the feelings came on with such strength and intensity that I was left powerless.

I was going to attempt to describe them, but why? For those that haven't repeatedly woken in a cold sweat, immersed in feelings of a nameless dread, words won't take your there.

Why? Because for the longest time that's just how it felt, and it was true for me in every sense of the word. I would see, feel, or remember something and it would "trigger" and set in motion an overwhelming flood of negative feelings that would completely consume me.

Normally, but not always, this happened in the dead of night, waking suddenly to intensely negative feelings. Feelings beyond those that I could describe or even want to try. Sweating, heart racing, it went on for months, off and on; and stretched to years. It lasted through most of my twenties

I told no one. Intuitively I thought no medication could help. Prayer? I wish. Or doctors, for that matter.

Nor did I want the stigma of being labeled a "nut" on my record to hamper future employment.

I could list more reasons why I told no one.

After one particular episode, I told myself I could no longer take these extreme swings of negativity. For the first time ever I contemplated... suicide. And it was that thought—that potential choice, the fact that after all these years another option/choice existed—which allowed me to ease the pressure off the other "trigger" of anxiety, panic, and despair, and gave me a sense of relief. From that moment on, bit by bit, I regained control of the present. Lost, however, were those past years of relationships and productivity.

These Days

I'm sure there are better and more efficient ways to come to a realization that help is available.

The quick answers we're looking for might not be readily available. But at least the direction to a more positive outcome could start to present itself.

Those initial steps could come in the form of VA health clinics, family, or NAMI (National Alliance of Mental Health), just to name a few.

This all took place before the letters PTSD became recognizable to the extent they are today. I suffered in silence, alone, never telling anyone.

CHAPTER 51

Dining out, Enemy cutlery

———◆———

NIGHT WAS FALLING, AND PREPARATION FOR THE
ambush was set—by a graveyard no less.

Claymores, trip wires, frags, willie peters—primed and ready to go
off. All the basic tools of an infantry squad were in place, and it was Sgt.
Raymond's rifle squad that lay in wait along the trail. They did not have to
wait for long. In that faint remaining light between sunset and complete
darkness, the shadows of approaching NVA could be seen.

Heartbeats instantly began to beat louder. No matter how well the
preparations were made in advance, in the chaos that is war, anything
could happen. That moment of transition from total quiet to total chaos
was near. As ambushes go, it was textbook. The NVA entered the Kill Zone,
and the overwhelming firepower from the combined explosives made
short work of those unfortunate enough to be caught in it. What wasn't
textbook was the unending screams of a mortally wounded NVA soldier
piercing the darkness. Unnerving and unsettling, they eventually stopped.
There was little sleep for the remaining night, until morning light was
available to check out the kill zone. When dawn came, Sgt. Raymond and
his squad cautiously went to inspect the damage. They found blood trails,
some weapons, and a rucksack—but no bodies? In disbelief, but not
uncommon in circumstances where adrenaline mixed with fear and panic,

coupled with an overwhelming survival instinct we all possess, those not critically wounded managed to drag their dead and wounded away.

Looking to salvage something of value from an abandoned enemy's rucksack, or at least a cool war souvenir of sorts, Sgt. Raymond opted for the practical choice of claiming a...spoon? Unlike the plastic ones issued to us that came and went in abundance with our C-rations, the NVA spoon that he held in his hands was slightly bigger than ours and made of metal with a Vietnamese/Chinese character stamped on it.

Well, Sgt. Raymond kept the spoon and still has it in his possession to this day. Not only that, but he used it in his day-to-day meals during the remainder of his tour in Vietnam.

"Ron," I asked him many years later, "Haven't you seen all those cooking shows about how the flavor of the food and eating experience can be enhanced by the presentation/plating and utensils in making a positive connection to the palate?" Speaking for myself (and as Ron told me, I'm not the first to express this), I would have chucked that spoon as far as it could go. Given the circumstances of its previous owner and his demise, the negative associations would be too much to have around as a visual and "taste" reminder. No thanks.

Ron lives not that far from me. We meet occasionally for lunch or at reunions. By chance, he joined up with Charlie Company within a month of my departure from Vietnam and we served with some of the same troops.

Below
Sgt. Ron Raymond's 'infamous spoon",

on one of his fatigue shirts from a later date.

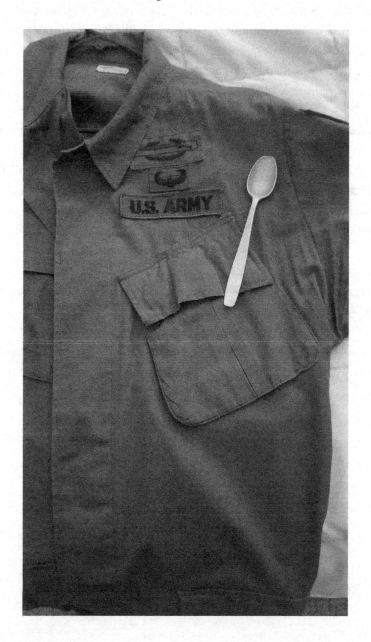

CHAPTER 52

Death with a Twist

---◆---

Location: Western Wyoming, many years since leaving Vietnam.

UP UNTIL NOW, I CONSIDERED MYSELF LUCKY TO HAVE never hit a deer, (or God forbid a moose or elk) given my countless miles of trucking throughout the lower forty-eight states and five Canadian Provinces as a long-haul trucker. It was a record of which I was proud and hoped to maintain. Unfortunately, smaller critters such as raccoons, possums, and squirrels didn't fare as well. Of course, it wasn't just luck but experience and the awareness of maintaining a safe speed, (sixty to sixty-five miles per hour) that helped me avoid many near misses. Bump it up to sixty-five miles per hour (mph) or greater will bag you many deer.

With that in mind, light snow was falling, the roads vacant for the most part, and I was now well into the night. Despite the fact that it would slow me down in the mountains, I was pleased to have my Semi maxed out at eighty thousand pounds, providing me with that extra needed traction. The rate of falling snow increased and my headlights now formed a tunnel in the white snow. I picked up the shape of a dark form directly on the road in front of me, in the middle of my lane no less—dead deer? Roadkill? Even on a dry clear road, it would have been chancy to attempt to go around it. I considered my alternative. My Kenworth tractor had a high ground clearance and I was confident my wheels could straddle over the possibly dead deer. Keeping my fingers crossed not to have my air lines ripped off, the decision was made; I was committed. Just before the moment of making the crossing, I was shocked! In the final fifty feet I saw the doe slowly rotate her dying body in my direction, extending her legs straight up in the air. Her head in a final twist, she looked straight at me, making me feel all the worse for what was about to happen. There was a thud and bumping sounds from my undercarriage as I hit the doe, as I completed what the initial vehicle failed to do. The truck was unharmed, but I was feeling bummed out.

To an outside observer, that preceding incident would in no way have a link to events in Vietnam—far from it. However, that whole scenario reconnected me with a memory from 'Nam.

It was in Vietnam, 1968, and we were pushing out from Firebase Bastogne towards the A Shau Valley. We made contact with NVA and the heavy firefight was well underway and undecided as of yet. We were held up by enemy bunkers out front. If you were foolish enough to stand up and look, you might be able to see them if looked hard enough. They were well camouflaged with the machine gun slits barely visible between the logs that formed the front of their bunker. The NVA were laying down long bursts of fully automatic fire that made any such action out of the question.

My buddy, Al Painter, edged up beside me. He was really bothered by a wound in his hand, and though it didn't appear all that big, it was causing him a lot of pain. I can't say the same for the dead NVA on the trail near us, who were riddled with bullets. Not minutes before, Zeke was making a move to step over a body. While doing so, he spotted a "Charlie buckle" on the dead NVA and made a move to claim it. Much like my dead deer from Wyoming, the "dead" NVA rolled over in a final twist and looked in the direction of Painter in a final gaze that was to haunt him. Thinking him a threat, another of our nearby troopers spotted the dying NVA's movement and put a burst into him, the blood splattering onto Zeke. Zeke was not at all pleased by being splattered with enemy blood and could be forgiven for considering it to be a bad omen.

He proved himself right by picking up a wound in his knee in that same firefight.

Zeke was sent to Japan for surgery and recovery and later back to the States to recover from his wounds on a cramped C-141 Starlifter, which in this case was modified as a flying air ambulance. Zeke and I reconnected at one of the 2/50 Deuce reunions and remain in touch. I'm sure to look him up whenever I'm in the Philadelphia, Pennsylvania area.

CHAPTER 53

Beam me up Scotty!
(the Future is here)

———◆———

LET ME CHANGE THE TOPIC FOR A BIT AND TAKE US TO 2019. We left the port of Southampton, England and it was the second day of our two-week journey to circumnavigate Great Britain including multiple stops in transit. It was a long overdue vacation with my wife. I woke up looking out the cabin window at the large ocean swells/waves hammering our cruise ship. I was somewhat mesmerized by the wind and waves, a few actually splashing against the window. It caused me some concern, but I was not overly worried, even though the ship had developed a slight chronic list. That thought overlapped with the fact that in a few days we were to stop in Belfast, Ireland, and had scheduled a tour for the Titanic exhibition. I put aside those negative feelings and left the cabin on a somewhat zigzagging walk looking for my sea legs to get my morning coffee.

The storm remained bad enough that it caused the Captain to reluctantly bypass our first port-of-call to the Channel Islands, off the northern coast of France. After all, we had the latest technology/radar and the ship's stabilizers were doing a fine job keeping me from getting seasick, which had been my main concern at the start of this voyage. It also reminded me of another disquieting thought. We were not far from the Isles of Scilly, the site of a naval catastrophe off the coast, near Cornwall, England. At roughly this location in 1707, in a similar storm, the British Navy lost some of its best men when four of their ships were smashed against rocks and reefs. Well over one thousand lives were lost—among them the British Admiral Shovell on the Flagship Association. That was a time when ships were a fraction of the size of today's vessels, without the benefit of engines, and were totally dependent on wind and sails. What they lacked most was critical navigation equipment. It all boiled down to finding the intersecting points of latitude and longitude, those horizontal and vertical intersecting lines that crisscross our globe. Finding one's latitude was a straightforward calculation. Longitude was the missing ingredient, and for that, a very accurate clock was key.

Determined not to let this happen again, the British Navy set up what you could think of as an R & D (Research and Development) Department to tackle the problem. It offered some serious money to whomever could design a working, reliable clock that could handle rough seas and harsh conditions with minimal maintenance over long periods. It took about seventy years, but eventually a very accurate timepiece known as a Marine Chronometer took the prize.

Here in the United States, our military has its own R & D branch. It goes by the acronym of DARPA, (Defense Advanced Research Projects Agency). You may be asking yourself, "Why have I never heard of them?" That's a good question. After all, they have been around since the late 1950s and have been instrumental in everything from the early development of the Internet, to the development of the M-16, and countless other projects designed to keep our military one or two steps ahead in the game of military.

DARPA first came to my attention when I happened to be reading an article in one of my favorite publications back in 2004—an issue of *Wired* magazine. It dealt with an upcoming event featuring a race between completely autonomous self-driving vehicles. The setting was the Mojave Desert, and the vehicles were lined up waiting for the starting gun. Actually, they looked more like a random collection taken from a junk yard, or demolition derby track, and cobbled together to do God-knows-what. Once they were off, it seemed to be a comedy rather than a serious undertaking. Some cars barely got out of the starting gate before conking out. In conjunction with major universities around the world, a prize of one million dollars was offered to any Remote Operating Vehicle that could complete a 150-mile course through a challenging variety of terrain. The fifteen starters were a mash-up of entrants that were selected from the best of the original prospects. None of them made it to the finish line, yet today we've arrived at a place where autonomous tractor-trailers complete cross-country trips and driverless cars are becoming a common feature.

From crossbows to muskets to automatic weapons to "phasers", the writing is on the wall, and in some respects the technology already exists to shrink the components that will put what would have been considered futuristic weapons into the hands of today's soldier. Rail-guns, laser weapons, weaponized drones, and more will have us all rethinking and going back to reconsider the Second Amendment. I suggest to those that haven't already, go to the DARPA website and check out the various projects they have listed—past, present, and future. Many of these projects encourage participation from the general public at large.

CHAPTER 54

"Those wonderful flying machines"

———————◆————

I THOUGHT IT WORTH MENTIONING MORE ABOUT AIR-
CRAFT IN GENERAL FOR MULTIPLE REASONS. FIRST, THEY
were such a big presence during my time in the military—before, during,
and after my Tour in Vietnam. I thought they deserved more explanation
and description.

During my tour with the 101st, we ranged over large parts of South
Vietnam and came in contact with a multitude of aircraft— either directly
with choppers of various kinds or having the opportunity to view and
observe them in action. Though warfare has been in existence for thousands of years, and mankind has been beating each other's brains out for all
that time, the introduction of aircraft brought a whole new level of destruction to the scene. I want to "bookend" a couple of aircraft that put into
perspective the advances made in a relatively short amount of time, involving the developments of airpower and warfare.

In WWI, one of the top line fighters was the Sopwith Camel. A
Biplane constructed of wood and fabric that had a top speed of 120 mph. I
used to make models of one as a kid using balsa wood and paper and glue
that wasn't much different than the actual ones. Its counterpart in Vietnam
would have been something like the F-4 Phantom, a fighter jet capable of
speeds of around seventeen hundred mph which packed a deadly mix of

armament, be they bombs or 20 mm cannons firing at a rate of six thousand rounds per minute.

All that took place in a span of less than fifty years! Between the creation of those two aircraft, a whole host of other flying critters made it on to the scene. Helicopters of all types with special capabilities, more jets, F-100s, and F-105s to name a few. Some aircraft were holdovers from WWII, such as the Douglas Sky-Raider, a single-prop fighter/bomber that made it ideal in some ways for close combat support, since it could fly slower and could better "eyeball" its targets and didn't have to rely on spotter aircraft to mark their targets.

BLACKBIRD

The SR-71 "Blackbird" spy plane was ultra-secret at the time and in many ways a class by itself. In so many ways, it was head-and-shoulders above anything else flying out there. With its futuristic sleek design, titanium skin, world record Mach 3+ speed capabilities, and altitude records, everything about it was cutting edge. Its operational altitude and speed made it untouchable and out of reach to enemy attack. To hammer home just how fast it was, I suggest you visit at a museum in Mobile, Alabama (Battleship Park). In one of their buildings, they have an SR-71 on display. Right below the nose and perpendicular to the Blackbird, you will see a glass-enclosed display case containing the Garand M1 infantry rifle along with a brief write-up of its capabilities. It was a very effective rifle used by American Infantry troops during WWII. It fired a .30-06 round. Its velocity is roughly 2,000 feet/second. If a .30-06 round from the Garand M1 and the SR-71 were to be in a race, all I can say is, put your money on the SR-71.

When I first caught a glimpse of it in Okinawa, the military would not admit to its existence. It was used by the CIA, and later by the US Air Force as they were flying many missions from there. It did most of its shooting with cameras and it did it well. It was by all accounts a one-of-a-kind aircraft and continued its work for many years.

Much of what it used to do is now done by satellites and with better results. Once more, all this in less than fifty years! We went from wood and fabric biplanes of WWI to the titanium skin of the Blackbird, all in that time period.

Where do motorcycles fit in with my time in Vietnam? Nowhere. Just the same, with my interest in motorcycles, and as the owner of a couple, I noticed the Henderson excelsior motorcycle, circa 1928 at the "Air Zoo" museum in Kalamazoo, Michigan. Some of its features caught my eye and brought it to my attention. It had a top end speed of over one hundred mph and its motor could be adapted for use in the Heath Parasol home-built airplane. The same plane with the same engine went on to win the 1924 Dayton International Air Race. Wow, how cool is that? You get two-for-the-price-of-one if you have one of these in your garage.

The "Boxcar," C-119

The Boxcar is named for its square boxcar shape. It is a smallish plane and on its last legs in terms of its service life, as it was even during my time in the Army. I found it to be a great jump plane in Jump School during my training as a paratrooper.

Even better is the civilian version (C-49) of the C-119 that appeared in the movie "Flight of the Phoenix" staring Jimmy Stewart, who served as a pilot during WWII. This movie deals with a plane that crashes in the desert and is reconstructed as sort of a "FrankenPlane." There are a couple scenes I love, one in particular where Jimmy Stewart discovers that a passenger who was key in the redesign/construction of the plane was a model aircraft designer and not a 'real' aircraft designer as he assumed. You have to watch it. Skip the remake, a second version that was filmed in 2004.

C-130, Troop transport and cargo aircraft

The C-130 is a very popular and reliable four-prop plane that has seen extensive duty and continues to do so. It was the plane in which I did the majority of my jumps while stateside before my deployment to Vietnam. While in Vietnam, it was used extensively in a variety of capacities. The tailgate in the rear allowed it to allow access to vehicles which could be driven right onto the tailgate, and even opened in mid-flight for airdrops. It was and is a "jack-of-all-trades" type of airplane that has ensured its long service. It remains in wide service today.

C-47, Douglass DC-3

What the C-130 was to Vietnam, the C-47 was to WWII. It became well-known in WWII as the aircraft dropping paratroopers of the 101st into Normandy during the invasion. Smaller in capacity with only two propellers, it made a name for itself in reliability and all-around ruggedness. I flew in one as a kid from Jakarta, Indonesia to Singapore. It provided our family with a mini-adventure as we traveled in the non-pressurized part of the cabin. (Just the men and boys. The women and babies sat in the front half in the pressurized section). During the Cold War, the C-47 participated in ferrying relief supplies at the time of the historic Berlin Blockade. It was a huge story in its day and is worthwhile knowing the drama that played out in the struggle between East and West.

While in the Saigon (now Ho Chi Minh City) during the Tet Offensive, I watched stream upon stream of red tracers weaving their way down from the air delivered by various gunships of ours at night. "Puff the Magic Dragon" is the name given to a C-47 modified into a gunship. It may well have been one of those raining down those tracers.

There are still a few C-47s kicking around today in various parts of the world, used by air freight companies. That speaks to its longevity and airworthiness, if nothing else. Not far from where I live, the Willow Run Air Museum has a restored C-47. The museum even offers rides to one and all for a modest price.

B-52 Bomber

Speaking of longevity, this baby is still around after all these years in a slightly modified manner. This is due mostly because of its avionics. It has a payload capacity to deliver huge amounts of bombs that would be roughly equal to fully loaded semi-trucks. A monster of a jet with eight engines, it had a very long-range flying capability. On many occasions, I saw them take off for their bombing missions in Okinawa, with heavy, dense black smoke spewing from their eight engines (much to the chagrin of the local Okinawan population). The B-52 Bomber has engines with a wingspan so large, one wing needs support on the ground when parked. It flew many bombing missions over areas of North and South Vietnam with deadly effects. Though reasonably accurate, you wouldn't want to be anywhere near when they lay down a string of their bombs.

C-141 Starlifter

The C-141 Starlifter is a large jet used for multiple purposes—everything from jumping paratroopers, (I did one jump from it) to basic troop transport and cargo. It also served as an air ambulance ferrying wounded American troops back to the US military bases such as at Dover, Delaware during the Vietnam War. I remember it as a cool and cutting-edge jet at the time, but now it has been replaced by the C-5 Galaxy and is no longer in service.

B-57 Canberra Bomber (2nd squadron of the Royal Australian Air Force)

Upon my arrival in Vietnam in September 1967, the main rear area base camp for the 1st Brigade of the 101st Airborne Division was located along the coast of the South China Sea at Phan Rang. Stationed along side us at the same base was a squadron of jet bombers belonging to the Australian Air Force, one of our allies at the time. I would see them take off and land a few times in the course of flying their sorties. Beyond that, we never had any interaction with them. Few people in the US are even aware of the participation, let alone the contribution, the Australians made as our Allies, which is a real shame.

Helicopters:

Huey, UH-1

In their standard configuration, Huey UH-1 could always be seen flying with their doors open, a door gunner on one side and the crew chief on the other, manning an M-60 machine gun.

They came in many stripes and colors, but without a doubt the one around which many military tactics changed and evolved has to be the UH-1. It was the predominant helicopter for the army in Vietnam. They proved themselves to be the ideal method of transport in a terrain that could otherwise be accessible only by foot. They would take us to the boonies to begin our operations and extract us from the boonies at the end of an operation, as well as keep us supplied with food, ammo, and other necessities while in the field. Gunship choppers (armed versions) were invaluable in supporting us through firefights.

Dustoff Hueys served as flying ambulances. They weren't armed with M-60s but that did not make them any less a target for enemy fire. So important and evolutionary were helicopters to military operations that the 101st Airborne Division is no longer a paratrooper Division and has been completely reorganized to reflect that reality. It has now been restructured and renamed the 101st Air Assault Division with a complete contingent of their own choppers.

Yes folks, no more parachuting out of planes for those guys. Now it is strictly all hopping and repelling out of choppers with the training designed to maximize those strengths.

AH-1G Cobra Gunships

The AH-1G came onto the scene in Vietnam as a gunship in 1967, specified and dedicated solely as an armed support helicopter. It didn't carry any troops or transport any supplies. It was manned by a pilot and copilot and that's all it needed to rain a concentrated amount of firepower to whatever happened to be in its sights. What it did have in spades were mini guns that could spew ungodly volumes of rounds, air to ground missile pods on each side, and an automated Grenade launcher.

Chinook CH-47

A powerful twin engine chopper, the Chinook CH-47 made its introduction in the 1960s and is a beast known for its carrying capacity and lifting capabilities. It could be loaded from the rear via a wide ramp or other side doors. It also had additional slings with hooks that were commonly used to carry artillery pieces/ammo to supply mountain top firebases. These slings were handy as a quick means of loading/unloading, which is critical in delivering supplies to forward combat areas in a minimal amount of time. It was common to see them going to and fro with supplies dangling from their undercarriage. That is why they were known to us by the loving name of "Sh*thooks". They usually had an M-60 machine gun mounted on each side, purely for defensive purposes.

Like the C-130, so successful were the Chinook's in their all-around performance that given a few upgrades in avionics, plus modifications in added composites, they continued in service well over fifty years after their introduction and remain a mainstay in the Army.

Sikorsky Sky Crane - (Flying Tow Truck), Yep, that's basically what they were. If heavy lifting or salvage work was required, this is who they called.

The Humble Cessna

Unlike the majority of military aircraft or any related pieces of equipment, camouflage and the avoidance of drawing enemy fire is an obvious key to survival, or so one would think.

Not so with these guys. They would often be used as spotter planes for the much faster jets and sometimes chopper gunships. They were on the lookout for enemy troop concentrations, bunkers, trucks, or anything that in their mind spelled "target". In doing so, they had to fly a fine line between drawing fire and avoiding being shot down themselves. If they found a target, the Cessna pilot would fire white phosphorus (WP) rockets to mark the spot for their "big brothers," the jets. The billowing white smoke from the WP rockets acted as a visual point from which the jets would then come screaming down and drop their bombs, make a strafing run with their 20 mm cannons, or both.

CHAPTER 55

Fletcher,
"The Yellow Brick Road"

SEPT 29,1967

The above date is well noted among us in Charlie Co., 2/502, 1st Brigade, 101st airborne division. On that day, I was descending down the stairs off a chartered Boeing 707 jet in Cam Ranh Bay, in Vietnam. In a couple of weeks, I would soon be inserted as a replacement along with a few others to join the above-named Charlie company, approximately three hundred miles north of me, to be assigned to the 3rd Platoon I'll be describing below. It was currently operating out in the boonies from its base camp in Chu Lai in the Northern I Corp. Clueless about what I had let myself in for, had I known, a plan B might have been in order.

On that same morning, Charlie Company finished a silent breakfast and Capt. Godboldte laid out the orders for the day. Charlie Company didn't have the luxury of stairs as they descended a mountainside loaded down by heavy rucksacks and weapons/ammo. A feeling of unease added to the weight they carried. Apprehension in making contact with the NVA was on everyone's mind. The night before, numerous campfires flickered from suspected enemy positions in the valley below. One of our company medics—Jesse "Doc" Partida—wanted to join with the third Platoon and see first-hand what was about to go down. It took a fair bit of convincing by his friend Homero Gomez (Fletcher's Radio Telephone Operator) to remain with the Captain at the command post. Homer's convincing won the day. It may have been well for Jesse that he stayed back.

Down the mountain Charlie Co. continued, 2nd Platoon followed by the 1st Platoon and then Fletcher's 3rd Platoon. Capt. Godboldte remained on top of the ridge line with the 4th Platoon. Eventually at the valley floor, the Company came across a "yellow brick road," a remnant of Vietnam's past as a French Colony. The road was constructed of cobblestones that took on its yellow hue from the pigment of the surrounding earth. This was not to be the "Yellow Brick Road" from the movie "The Wizard of Oz" that led to all good things. No, nothing good was to come by traveling on this "yellow brick road". In single file, the 2nd Platoon proceeded down the road followed by the 1st Platoon. Rice paddies and dense vegetation bordered the road. Traveling such a road held both a blessing and a curse. Nothing is better for a foot soldier than to have an easy, unobstructed path in terms of getting from A to B without having to hack their way through jungle undergrowth. Conversely, nothing is worse from the standpoint of the exposure to being ambushed from bunkers and spider holes that could conceal the all-but-invisible weapons lying in wait. And yes, they were waiting.

The NVA opened up with all they had, laying down a deadly field of fire into the 2nd Platoon. The shock, chaos, and confusion of being subjected to such an intense ambush is something that can't be described unless you are unfortunate enough to experience it. AK-47s, RPG rocket launchers, RPD machine guns, and crisscrossing green tracers killed some outright, wounded others, and sent everyone else into a prone position finding cover by any means they could. For many, that meant diving into a mix of mud and water mingled with water buffalo s**t that formed rice paddies that made fertile ground for rice plants and the opposite for those trapped there. Leave aside the fact that this soup of mud and waters is the last thing into which you want to drop your weapon/ammo. The 3rd Platoon, led by Fletcher, was just far enough back to avoid being caught in the hell to which the 2nd and 1st Platoons were being subjected. It was under such conditions that only a front-line soldier like Fletcher could see what needed to be done. On his initiative, he made a decision to take the 3rd platoon and circle around to the rear of the NVA positions and relieve the 2nd Platoon and 1st Platoon from their dire straits.

Immediate is a relative term in this case. With as much speed and caution as he could muster, Fletcher led the 3rd Platoon through a series of two rice paddies—each over one hundred yards wide—and assorted heavy brush that flanked the NVA leading to their rear positions. These rice paddies offered plenty of chances for Fletcher's Platoon to themselves be caught in the open. To lessen the risk, the M60 machine guns were brought to secure covering fire as his 3rd Platoon troops crossed the rice paddies if an ambush were to happen.

With one rice paddy behind them, and with some security of vegetation providing cover, the 3rd Platoon hung a right only to find they would have to cross yet another rice paddy similar to the first. Repeating the process, they used in crossing the first two rice paddies, they eventually crossed without incident to slightly higher ground. The 3rd Platoon had now reached a point that placed them behind the ambush site, but still with some ground yet to cover. While waiting for the rear squad to catch up with the main body of the 3rd Platoon, Sgt. Fletcher glanced to his right and was taken aback to see two NVA .51 cal. heavy machine guns in a fairly close position. One alone would have been disastrous, but two together could have chewed through the 3rd Platoon in no time flat. What they lacked though was any NVA manning them. To go check them out or not? The bigger priority remained helping the 2nd and 1st Platoon out of their "kill zone". Fletcher gathered his platoon and pushed on, putting some distance between the 3rd Platoon and those .51 cal.

With the distance between the 3rd Platoon and the main ambush site closing, the tension increased as imminent contact could take place at any time. With Sp/4 Bob Britt walking point, that time came soon enough as he came face to face with an NVA soldier coming the other way.

They exchanged fire, with the NVA getting hit. If they didn't know it before, the jig was up as the NVA became aware they were being approached from the rear. At this point, Fletcher's 3rd Platoon could expect to be fully engaged at any moment. Who will spot whom first?

Approximately one hundred yards ahead, the lead squad noticed a communication phone line across the trail. Following it to its source revealed an enemy bunker. Our trooper who discovered it turned to pass on his find and it was at this moment that he took a hit and was wounded. Another one of our troopers eliminated the bunker with a frag. Seconds later, another NVA and his AK-47 in a separate position was taken out by one of our squad leaders, Sgt. Balog. The intensity of the fighting was now at a level on par with those caught in the initial ambush. Out of nowhere, a burst of automatic weapons fire ripped into Fletcher's left ammo pouch on his waist, another round hitting his wallet in his left breast pocket. Miraculously, he remained unharmed. Fletcher fired off a full clip into a dense area of trees/brush from where he thought the enemy lay, then backed up and regrouped to an "aid station" where our medic, "Doc" Treese (himself wounded), was caring for the mounting number of our wounded.

Meanwhile, Acting Platoon Sgt. Burns was having it out with an enemy position some fifteen yards from the aid station. He threw a frag into the position, then turned to face Fletcher. Burns was hit by enemy fire. Fletcher was able to walk up and pull Burns out of the line of fire. Working along with his RTO, Homer Gomez, they managed to drag him to the aid station, but not before Burns was shot one more time. With the pins pulled on a frag in one hand, and the other containing a Willie Peter (white phosphorous grenade), Fletcher charged the bunker and tossed the WP into the bunker that has caused the wounding of Sgt. Burns. He heard rapid slapping as the NVA inside hopelessly tried to smother the white phosphorus burning throughout his body. Fletcher then followed that by dropping a frag in after it. The following explosion could well be seen as an act of mercy, given the painful burns of white phosphorus.

Coming up on another enemy position, Fletcher saw three of our troopers preparing to assault it, one PFC Frank Aragon indicated into which he was prepared to crawl. Fletcher had him back off, since something was suspicious about the entrance. Sure enough, it had two bamboo poles rigged with 60mm mortar rounds set to explode when tripped. Fletcher "smoked the frag" and tossed it into the entrance eliminating it as a threat. Just the same, he told PFC Aragon to wait a few minutes before attempting to go in.

With that threat contained, Sgt. Fletcher went to see if he could try and link up with the 2nd squad, which he assumed was roughly fifty yards to his front, just past a hedgerow. He gave the order to one of his NCOs to hold the platoon where it was. Fletcher set out and crossed an open area about fifty yards wide and slipped through a break in a hedgerow. This put him in a triangular hedgerow complex with an open area. Once more risking exposure, he crossed this open area that terminated in higher ground. Scanning the area below him, Fletcher could see five or six NVA fighting positions dug into a rice paddy drain at the base of bank. These positions were abandoned, but a great deal of expended ammo casings littering the surrounding area told their own story. Not more than one hundred-plus yards to their front is where the 1st and 2nd Platoon lay pinned down.

Having cleared these positions to his satisfaction, Fletcher then turned to his right rear and cut through another break in yet another hedgerow. He came to a sudden halt after spotting a GI laying alone about five yards past the hedgerow in an open area somewhat hidden by a small tree, with just enough grass to provide concealment. As Fletcher moved towards him, the GI turned to raise his head. Fletcher recognized him as Pfc. George Overshine with the 2nd squad. Luckily, he was still alive and uninjured. Unaware of the immediate danger he was facing, Sgt. Fletcher continued his move towards Overshine. Overshine began crawling three or four feet to his right front, exposing his position while pointing out an enemy position. In that split second, Overshine was hit with a burst of automatic weapons fire, killing him instantly. Not hesitating, Fletcher ran through the hedgerow, leaped over his body, and rolled into a firing position. What he saw was the enemy gunner trying to get his gun down into his position. He shot the gunner twice, and the NVA sunk into his hole. Fletcher later told me that he feels Overshine saved his life in pointing out the hidden NVA.

The fighting was far from over. The intensity of the engagement increased again with Fletcher now taking fire from his left front. Calling out to where he thought the 2nd squad was, Fletcher yelled for supporting covering fire and got no response. In another bold move, Fletcher pulled the pin on a frag and moved forward, firing in the direction of the enemy position. He let the handle fly from the frag and on the count of three thousand, tossed it at the NVA position, maintaining fire until detonation.

Chalk up one more NVA and his AK-47.

While reloading, Fletcher spotted another enemy soldier on a hillside behind the 1st and 2nd Platoon. Fletcher hit him with a couple rounds and again removed yet one more enemy threat. Pulling back somewhat, and not wanting to fire in the direction of the 1st or 2nd Platoon, Fletcher noticed an enemy position that was empty but still contained a usable machine gun. Fletcher disabled it by firing some rounds into the machine gun. He then checked another bunker and found it empty. Finally seeing someone from the 2nd squad down the trail, Fletcher assumed the area was clear. More rifle fire was heard back at the main body of the 3rd Platoon and Fletcher eased back to the reconnect and spent the balance of the day aiding the evacuation of the dead and wounded and getting topped off with much needed ammo and supplies. He then consolidated the 3rd Platoon's position, now having broken the grip of the NVA on this day.

The preceding accounts dealt primarily with one individual and rightly so. It was Fletcher's leadership and exploits that day which were key in saving most of the 3rd Platoon as they battled their way through enemy positions against high odds to relieve the pressure off of the 2nd and 1st Platoons and bring Charlie Company to a safe conclusion. Most of the 1st and 2nd Platoons by this time were out of ammo and in imminent danger of being overrun.

It was on that basis that Sgt Fletcher was awarded the Distinguish Service Cross for Bravery, our nation's second highest award for valor by General Goodpasture.

Bob Britt

Wounded, bandaged, and awaiting medivac, Sp/4 Britt. still had his wits about him as he scanned the perimeter of the makeshift aid station, despite the pain from his wounds. His eye was drawn to a slight discoloration in the leaves in some underbrush that appeared different than when he first saw it. Not having his M-16 available, he motioned to Sgt. Balog that they should go over and investigate. Getting closer, Bob's suspicions were correct. An enemy soldier was revealed in a spider hole with an AK-47. Unarmed as he was, Bob contemplated jumping in the hole and getting himself a POW. Not taking any chances, Sgt. Balog put a burst in the Charlie, eliminating him as a threat and coming close to hitting Bob in the process.

As the above showed, the surrounding area was still far from secure, but the wounded were piling up and ammo was getting low. The Battalion commander Danford, who was circling overhead along with other choppers, made the call to drop down and kick some of the desperately needed ammo out the door.

Next, a "dustoff chopper" descended and Bob had his fingers crossed to find a space on this one. Hovering, the noise and wind from the swirling dust, as well as the exposure, made it imperative to get out of there ASAP. As Bob slid onto floor of the chopper, the Huey pilot wasted no time and increased the revs to gain altitude and get the hell out of there. The "dust-off" medic moved towards Bob, preparing to attend to his wounds. That was not to be because AK rounds tore into the chopper, hitting the medics knee, another shattering his arm, leaving little intact to hold it on, resulting in a massive loss of blood. The medic rapidly went into shock.

Looking to see the source of the fire, Bob turned and was stunned to see an NVA soldier no more than sixty yards away, reloading another clip in an attempt to bring down the chopper. It made for a frantic/desperate situation as Bob looked around to reach for medic's M16, held in a rack. Unfortunately, it too was a casualty, having been destroyed by an AK round. Shouting to the pilot without luck, Bob tried to get his attention above all the noise and have him pass back his '45. His yelling went unheard. Still, the pilot did manage to get airborne and headed to safer skies, a miracle in itself.

Now out of range of enemy weapons, the tables were turned as Bob became the medic, and the medic the patient. He managed to put a tourni-quet on the medic and stem the heavy loss of blood. In keeping with pro-cedure, Bob marked a 't' on the medic's forehead using his blood. This was to alert medical staff on arrival that a tourniquet was in place. Not feeling all that well himself with his wounds, Bob managed to remain conscious.

Homer Gomez

Homer was Sgt. Fletcher's RTO on September 29 and was instru-mental in helping many wounded back to a makeshift aid station, monitor-ing the communication between the Charlie Co's captain and Colonel Danford. He also did more than his share of the fighting throughout the whole ordeal that day. It's difficult to put on a scale the burden combat places on different individuals, both during and at later moments of their life. I can say that Homer has borne much and given a lot to his country. Later to become Sgt. Gomez, he was my squad leader at one point.

I find it troubling that in his home region of South Texas where he lives and the whole border region stretching to California for that matter, many good Americans have to prove over and over as they go about their daily lives that they are indeed "real Americans". Whether from the inconvenience of the many routine border patrol stops at various checkpoints, or the general hysteria brought about in what is seen as securing our southern border, it does a big disservice to one and all.

One danger in describing events as I've done is that they may appear to have taken place in quick succession, when the opposite is the case. Many intense mini-firefights are taking place simultaneously. It is difficult to try to sort out some sort of coordination in all the chaos while your own life is under constant threat—not just with dying, but in facing death in brutal and savage ways. At the end of such a day, many more enemy dead lay about than what we suffered. That is little comfort to anyone who has lost the connection to irreplaceable friends and comrades no matter how big or small the body count.

In such circumstances, having a person in charge at the ground level in terms of leadership with the courage to make things happen is all the difference. Sgt Fletcher was one of the few who had the rare mix of physical and psychological skills/blend to carry out what needed to be done. This was seen not just on that day, but throughout his three tours in Vietnam and subsequent career of over twenty-six years in the army. Many years later, while visiting at his home, I asked Fletcher—of all his service tours in the Army, what outfit did he consider the best to have led. He said it was the 3rd Platoon of Charlie Co. 2/502, 1st Bde, 101st Airborne. I'm glad our tours overlapped while he was there leading the 3rd Plt. Most of us who served with him felt a void in leadership when he left after that first tour. I could go on and on about Sgt. Fletcher's various exploits both before and after his tours in Vietnam, but I no doubt would be well into another book.

Above
S.Sgt. Fletcher, being awarded his Distinguished Service Cross for Valor
by General Andrew Goodpasture for the firefight that took place on
Sept. 29, 1967.

Below
Fletcher's display case showing the numerous awards
acquired over the course of his 26+ year career in the army.
Upon retirement he held the rank of Command Sergeant
Major, the highest rank could one attain as an NCO.

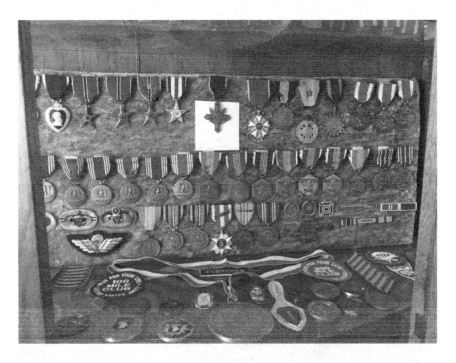

Above
Close up of one section of the display case.

The Distinguished Service Cross is front and center on the top row.

I gave thought to itemizing and listing all the various medals/decoration/awards shown here, then I threw my hands up when I realized I would be well into writing another book.

Some of the key ones: the Distinguished Service Cross for Valor, Combat Infantryman Badge, Purple Hearts, numerous Jump Wings, Army Ranger tabs and the medals for valor are displayed here.

Below
Good pic of Homer Gomez in this badass pose.

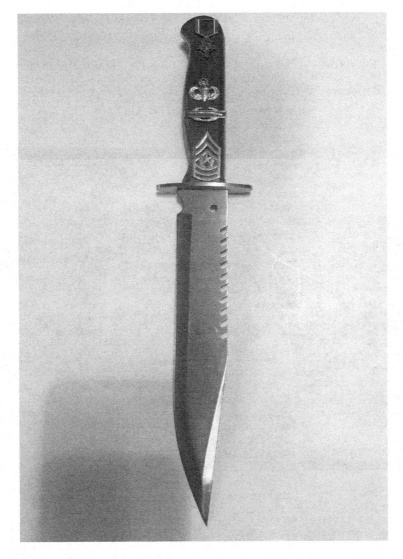

Above
Bob Britt and this knife made for Fletcher in 2019 and presented it to him on behalf of those of us in the 3rd Platoon, Charlie Co. 2/502.

Below
Taken at Jesse (Doc) Partida's home in Texas
after attending his 50th wedding anniversary.

Front row – left to right, Homer Gomez, Pete Major, Bob Britt

Back row- left to right, Jesse's grandson (Zachary), Mike Perry, Jesse Partida, Jerry Garcia, Dan Perry

CHAPTER 56:

Altar Boy

———◆▬◆———

I GUESS I WAS ABOUT TEN AT THE TIME AND IT'S NOT something for which I volunteered. I think my mom put my name in the ring without any input from my end. I'm talking about being an altar boy. Mass at our local Catholic Church was conducted in Latin in those days. I can safely say that the study and memorization of Latin wasn't high on my list of priorities. The priest was Dutch, and with English as his second language, that didn't make the lessons any easier. There were some parts of the Mass I liked that made the job better—ringing the smaller hand bells at the altar before Communion, also a cue to me that the Mass was drawing to a close, the smell of burning incense during Mass which I found comforting and pleasant. The best part for me was ringing the large Steeple Bells in the back of the Church. This was done by reaching as high as I could, then pulling down on the rope that would dangle from the steeple bells. Doing so would lift my body clear off the ground as the bells swung back and forth. I loved that part of it, like a reverse bungee jump.

We lived in Indonesia at the time, a chain of over three thousand islands near the equator on the island of South Sumatra, in a compound called Sungai Gerong, next to Standard Vacuum Oil Refinery. The time was in the mid-to-late 1950s. It was a very exotic place to be, which is true even now for that matter. People here in the west might come across Indonesia in the news as a tourist destination (i.e., Bali, Jakarta), or sometimes associate it with massive earthquakes and tsunamis that can wreak havoc, not to mention volcanoes, of which many active ones exist.

It is worth noting that Indonesia is the largest Muslim country in the world in terms of population. Though generally moderate, there is an extreme element, and the Christian minority has to tread carefully.

My father worked for Standard Oil as a shift supervisor and our family came along for the ride. My three siblings, plus the addition of one born there, made us a family of five kids.

It has been said that travel in itself is an education and I must say I agree. In our total of four years there, we soaked up a lot of lessons in geography, world cultures, cuisines, weather patterns, languages, and more. By the time we relocated to North America, I had no problem holding a conversation in Indonesian, thanks in large part to our servants. Yep, servants! Though not rich by any stretch of the imagination, Indonesia was such a poor country in terms of its economy then and now, that all the foreign families employed at least one to three servants, some living with us in attached servant quarters. It wasn't Downton Abbey, but it certainly spoiled the heck out of me when it came to doing any house chores. To add to my less-than-diligent work habits, our school days ended early (12:30 pm) due to the high heat in that part of the world. We lived less than one hundred miles from the equator and our air conditioning was always underpowered and overworked, being no match for the heat and humidity. We had two seasons, dry and monsoon.

To my detriment, I was often able to convince my mom that I had completed my homework (not!) and off I'd go to the local community pool which was the focus of activity for us kids. Unbelievable as it might sound, we had access to an Olympic size fifty-meter pool with a three-meter springboard, construction of which was completed during our second stint there.

The primarily American and Canadian foreign workers employed by Standard Oil lived in a high fenced-off compound that separated us from the greater local population of Indonesians. It was a separation brought about that defined both the extremes of poverty and wealth, foreign and local. It was also for security purposes. Indonesia was politically unstable during those days. As such, we had a company of Indonesian soldiers bivouacked not far from our house. Some of us kids would sneak over to their barracks where we were very impressed by all their weapons. They were a big step up from our BB guns. Usually the soldiers would shoo us away, however one time we talked them into letting us hold a machine gun. I recall thinking how heavy it was. Another thing that stuck with me was that their helmets and uniforms were American issued.

Indonesia had recently regained their independence in more ways than one. During WWII it was occupied by the Japanese. With the war over, and ridding themselves of that burden, they went on to kick their Dutch masters out and gain independence from what until that time was known as the Dutch East Indies. Heavy concrete fortification and bunkers could still be seen here and there, a reminder of the harsh Japanese occupation. As a former paratrooper myself, I was later surprised to learn that the same refinery my dad worked at was taken over in WWII by a battalion of Japanese Paratroopers.

The Dutch were no longer in power from a colonial standpoint, but they still kept a strong economic grip operating Dutch Shell Oil, situated just up the river from us.

Vietnam

Less than ten years after my days in Indonesia, I returned to that region of the world as a soldier with the 101st Airborne Division, to find myself operating out in the boonies not far from our base camp along the coast of the South China Sea by Chu Lai. My twenty-first birthday was approaching, and no one was planning to throw me a party. Still, our resupply moments in the boonies always made it feel like a bit of a party with us stocking up on food and other goodies.

On this occasion, a lull in the action made it okay to allow an infrequent visit to the field by one or our Army clergy, in this case a Catholic priest. The Choppers had been coming and going—noise, dust, and the constant uncertainty of being shot. It was all business. In classic war zone fashion, a makeshift altar of ammo crates and C ration boxes would be quickly set up. There was no time for all the ritual and ceremony that surrounded me during my time as an altar boy. It was to be a ten-minute Mass, if that. Mass would be said in an abbreviated record time with the need to have it completed before the last chopper booked out. The priest would also take this occasion to hand out rosaries, the beads constructed of knotted string which many of us gladly took and wore around our necks—Catholics and non-Catholics alike. The visits in the Chu Lai area would alternate between the Catholic priest and a Protestant minister. One distinction I noticed was the Protestant minister carried a 45-cal. sidearm on his visits out in the field whereas the Catholic Priest didn't carry any weapon. I always viewed that as a reflection on the degree of faith between the two. There was no Rabbi though, for my lone Jewish buddy, Zeke, he had to pray extra hard until Hanukkah. However, his prayers were rewarded by being allowed to attend Jewish services in the rear area over Christmas while we remained in the boonies. His luck continued and he was able to stretch out his stay in the rear a few more days and kick back a bit. More power to him. I would have done the same myself. As to Muslim clergy, I can't recall there ever being any at the time, or any troopers of the Islamic faith in our company in any event.

As for the religious demographic in Vietnam, almost half the citizens practice some type of folk religion, then comes Buddhism, and after that a small segment of Catholics, established there during its occupation as a French colony.

CHAPTER 57:

Please Check Your Crossbows at the Door

———————◆———————

THAT'S RIGHT FOLKS, EVEN IN THE MIDDLE AGES WE had gun control of sorts—a dirty phrase in today's lexicon. During the twelfth century, crossbows and to a lesser extent longbows, were looked upon as an evil by most of the knights and nobility of the time who fought fully armored and were greatly put off by the fact that any lowly serf with a bit of training could upset that advantage with the use of armor piercing bolts fired from crossbows. Europe was mostly Catholic at the time and the collective royalty pleaded their case to the Supreme Court of the day— Pope Innocent II. The year was 1139 at the 2nd Lateran Council and Pope sided with the royalty in his decision and abandon went into effect. (Note: Muslims and Jews were excluded). It wasn't long before crossbows were once again being used with lethal effect and killing went on as usual.

Move up in time another six hundred years or so to the time of the American Revolution in 1776. The battlefield weapon of choice was the "Brown Bess", a flintlock musket that wasn't known for any great accuracy and you were doing well if you could get off two to three shots in a minute. That's on a good day in good weather. It wasn't the type of weapon one had to fear in terms of "drive by shootings", let alone mass shootings. Weapons manufacture during that era was largely a cottage industry with a general lack of standardization. It was in that setting with little concept of what lay ahead that the Second Amendment was adopted. If they had their crystal balls handy, a better selection of words and phrasing might have produced less conflict in our present times. It's not their fault. Heck, just to write the Constitution of the United States without once mentioning slaves or slavery took the best verbal gymnastics of the time. Going back to a general description of "arms", terms like semi/fully automatic, large capacity ammo clips/mags, silencers, laser scopes, tasers, stun guns, 3D printed guns, and "bump stocks" had yet to appear on the scene. I've not even mentioned the more exotic fare of weaponized drones, rail guns and the like.

A quick reading of the Second Amendment, if anything, adds to the confusion with its vague and ambiguous wording. The twenty-seven words contained in that one amendment reflect the mindset of a vastly smaller geographical collection of colonies comprised of a total population of roughly four million people. Put that up against our nation today, stretching from sea to sea with a population of over three hundred twenty-five million. That is just about 1.3% of today's population. My opinion on the matter sits somewhere in the middle (or so I'd like to think). I feel fully automatic weapons and large capacity clips/magazine have no place in our day-to-day surroundings. I could even go without handguns, but I don't have the energy to argue that point. Originally from Canada, and growing up watching the Winter Olympic, one my favorite sports to view is the Biathlon, a dual event combining cross-country skiing interspersed with target shooting. If you need more than that, well, we have hockey sticks, don't we?? The United States' role in the Vietnam War stretched from 1965 to 1975. It saw deaths in excess of a 55,000 on the U.S. side alone. Currently, there are thirty thousand gun-related deaths annually here in the U.S.! Sadder are the number of people willing to accept and live with so many needless deaths.

Look to the transportation industry as an analogy, and the trucking industry in particular. Should you ever find yourself close enough to a semi-tanker truck hauling something like anhydrous ammonia and catch a whiff of it seeping out of its escape value, you could be forgiven for gagging and having your lungs seize up. That or a whole host of other nasty chemicals and products such as sulphuric acid, chlorine gas, hydrochloric acids, nuclear waste, bulk pesticides, explosives, poisons, or countless other dangerous chemicals are spilling across highways or down your driveway for that matter. It wasn't always that way, but we have now come to our senses and the above goods now require proper labeling and matching paperwork to identify and list steps required should an emergency arise. I easily recall a time when regulations varied from state to state, and it was a simple matter to circumvent the law by getting an out-of-state license. DUIs and drug offenses remained hidden until the Department of Transportation (DOT) got everyone on the same page and a national CDL/HazMat system was put into place to erase those old loopholes. Failure to do so could result in big fines and possible jail time. Common sense, right! We then return to weapons of all descriptions, here are items specially designed to kill, maim, and wreak havoc and it's an uphill battle many times to get some consensus on the most basic regulations. There is no way to know if the person passing you on the street, though they might have a legally acquired a firearm, could be suffering from or capable of the following:

psychopathy, suffering from mental illness, suicidal, untrained in basic firearm handling, clumsy, a second away from road rage, unsafe or improper storage of firearms, dealing with dementia, in an abusing relationship, or lacking in maturity. To those we can add our garden variety crooks, drug dealers, felons, terrorists, and mass killers. To repeat a statistic, it's no wonder here in the US we suffer from over thirty thousand gun related deaths a year. Just another statistic until you or a close friend/family member is killed/injured. In less than two years we suffered more killed in the US alone than our whole time in Vietnam. All this takes place in a county that is supposedly at peace ?

EPILOGUE–
AKA, Not Quite Yet!

OR IS IT?

Given the nature of the material, time constraints, countless other considerations, or just plain wanting to wrap it up...I couldn't fit it all in. Including:

- The hours of boredom on guard.

- The gray areas of activity on military camps: black market, pimps, prostitution, hustlers.

- What-if choices.

- The politics of war.

- Friendly fire deaths (now there's an oxymoron for you!).

Friendly fire could happen in many ways, and what ends on the paperwork of a GI's death certificate as a KIA (killed in action) could be a long way from the actual facts of the case.

The more common cases of friendly fire would be the tragic instances of one squad on patrol walking into an ambush set up by a neighboring platoon. Given the inaccuracy of maps and the denseness of the jungle, and the noise and confusion, these events proved to be too common. And there was the close support from artillery fire and mortars. The NVA and us were almost on top of each other in many firefights, and calling in Artillery from what could be miles away, the rounds landing oftentimes yards from our positions. I was always amazed with the accuracy given the conditions. Still with "short rounds," rounds falling short of their intended target, casualties were bound to result.

It's not admitted in so many words, but different military units had varying levels of skill, training, and discipline, which resulted in more friendly fire cases. Luckily for the 101st, I like to think that we were better in those areas.

What goes for Artillery applies in spades when it comes to close air support. Jets skimming the treetops at a mind-blowing speed and dropping HE bombs, napalm, strafing with 20-mm cannons, Gunship choppers, rockets, 6,000-rpm mini-guns…I mean, what do you expect? Of course it can and will happen!

Or Trooper A leaves his safety off and accidentally shoots Trooper B. Don't get me started! I swear, every time we returned from the Boonies, someone hadn't cleared their weapon properly and a round went off!

The year's passage of time since the initial publication of this book has seen changes that, if anything, reflect and make more acute the urgency to wrap up this book and send it out to the world.

My brother Brian (see chapter 49) passed away not too long after the first printing in 2018. That loss in addition to me now sitting in one of the epicenters of the Coronavirus pandemic, (Detroit) has intensified, but not without difficulty, the need to get my book to print.

Glossary

Definitions, Acronyms:

P-38-

A very basic, but efficient manual can opener used to open C Ration cans. Pull tabs were nonexistent in those days (even for beer cans). This tiny but critical piece of hardware fit the bill perfectly to get into our all-important food supplies.

*R.E.M.F.'s, Rear Echelon M****r F*****r's-*

An all-inclusive term to describe those in the rear areas (usually the larger, permanent base camps that contribute to making our lives more miserable than necessary in one regard or another.

NVA-

for North Vietnamese Army, North Vietnam's Regular Army Troops.

Viet Cong-

communist guerrilla troops in South Vietnam, could be anyone, as they were not in uniform and in one degree of another were interspersed among the local population.

Negroes, Blacks -

Two terms that have been reversed in terms of their commonly acceptable usage of their day. In the 1960s, negro was the predominant word in describing the black population. This fell into disfavor to be replaced by the current term, Afro-American.

Punt/bunt gun-

Sort of a cross between a "shotgun" and a cannon, used to shoot waterfowl in large numbers with one shot. Now banned in the United States but not before massive numbers of ducks were killed.

Nose Art-

The general term for the personalized art work and markings that were put on the "nose" of helicopters and other aircraft during the Vietnam war and other wars. Sometimes these art pieces were a little too explicit for the "brass" and were censored. A great example of the "pic" on the nose of the chopper is a photo with Homer Gomez standing in front.

C.I.B.-

(Combat Infantryman's Badge), awarded to those Army soldiers with an Infantry Military Operation Specialty who have been in combat.

Some Euphemisms:

Collateral Damage-

Usually meant to describe the killing of civilians, unintentional or not. If you can't come to terms with describing something despicable the next best thing is to give is a sweet sounding, innocuous name.

Lethal Autonomous Weapons-

The sanitized term for "killer robots". This sounds much better. It is a fast-growing field. The whole area or robotics lends itself extremely well to weaponization and even ones created with an entirely different purpose in mind can often be adapted to military use of one sort or another. Check out Boston Robotics. Drones were already established in this field and evolving rapidly.

LBJ-

(not, Lyndon Baines Johnson, President at the time)

a.k.a. Long Bin Jail... Military stockade that contained US soldiers for various infractions. Located in the Saigon vicinity. Notorious for the harsh conditions in which many prisoners were treated.

Cluster F**k –

Very often heard and meant to describe a gathering/clustering together of usually three or more troops that exposes them to maximum casualties which could be inflicted by mortars, bursts of automatic weapon fire, mines, etc. A common usage is, "break up that Cluster F**k", which translated means, "Spread out, assholes, or you'll get yourselves all killed".

RPD/RPG-

Don't be confused, RPG stands for rocket propelled grenade (launcher). Let me tell you, it is more "rocket" than grenade, judging by the size of it. RPD is a machine gun used by the NVA— deadly, effective, and scary!

Killed by "Small Arms Fire"-

The term "small arms fire" leaves one with the impression that it's a "low-cal" way of dying. Make no mistake. A "burst" of smalls arms could just as easily blow your head off or take down a Chopper.

Some Museums to Consider:

There are countless museums related to the Vietnam War and wars in general. Here are a few I checked out.

Willow Run Airport, Detroit, Michigan-

Close to where I live. During WWII it was the largest bomber plant in the world, building B-17s and B-24s.

Ft. Wayne, Detroit, Michigan-

I boarded a train and left Detroit bound for Ft. Knox, Kentucky, the first stop to begin my three-year enlistment in the Army. It's pretty run down and neglected at the moment, though I've heard it will be getting a face lift soon.

Battleship Park, Mobile, Alabama-

A nice assortment of aircraft, the SR-71 included, a submarine and yes, a battleship. I wouldn't mind visiting this museum again.

101st Airborne Museum, Ft. Campbell, Kentucky -

They have upgraded the museum there and I was impressed with the little I was able to glimpse.

Smithsonian, National Air and Space Museum
Near Washington Dulles International Airport; Washington, D.C. at the
Steven Udvar-Hazy Center-

A great collection of aircraft covering everything from bi-planes to the
Space Shuttle and rockets and satellites. The last SR-71 to fly is now on display here. I highly recommend a trip here. Take more than a day to take it
all in—and it's free! (Almost. They get you on the parking fee).

General Custer Museum, Monroe, Michigan-

Some good information on General Custer beyond his well know participation and last stand at the Battle of Little Big Horn. Going through the
main entrance is an actual "punt gun" that I described earlier. It's HUGE!

Air Zoo, Kalamazoo, Michigan-

Another good museum with a wide variety of aircraft about a couple of
hours from where I live. I specifically went there to see the SR-71.

Henry Ford Museum, Dearborn, Michigan-

World famous. It contains a revolving series of displays, some of which
have a historical connection with various wars.

National Museum of Nuclear Science and History-
Albuquerque, New Mexico

The name says it all. Very good museum. I'm ready for a return trip.

Titan Missile Museum, near Tucson, Arizona-

Some scary things to reflect on here in case you missed the Cold War.
Sadly, I think we're heading back to those times. Good museum, I'd like to
make it back here also.

Arromanches, Normandy, France-
French town on Gold/Juno Beach

On one of the beachheads of the British/Canadian landing sites in Normandy during D-Day in WWII. Nice displays, videos, and gift shops. Lots of shops/restaurants in the town of Arromanches itself.

Books and Libraries to Consider (in no particular order):

I've always loved reading. We didn't have access to television until I was about twelve, interspersed with the odd movie. When I was young ALL books were hardcopy only and we read them the old fashion way, using our eyeballs while clutching some form of printed matter in our hands. Now, many more options are available to sponge up the wealth of material around us— eBooks, video, podcasts, and audio books. There is no excuse, people, use any format—read! Not only that, but costs have dropped dramatically, and access has increased exponentially.

Plymouth Public Library-

One of my offices away from home. It allows me a quiet spot without distractions (such as our dog barking!) and a place to focus. Their cozy fireplace in the winter is a plus and great place to mellow out. There is lots of help within an arm's reach if I need it.

The Library Book by Susan Orlean – (author of *The Orchid Thief*)

Centers around the 1986 fire in the Los Angeles Public Library and libraries/books as a whole.

Library of Congress, Washington, DC-

Books, books, and more books - but, not just books. They also have maps, videos, and media information stored in a variety of formats.

University of Texas, Lubbock Texas-

The only University in the United States that has a department devoted to the Vietnam War.

1984 by George Orwell-

At the time I read it, the date "1984" was still in the future. It's also the title of the book itself. It was written back in 1949 and tells of a futuristic totalitarian government where life was okay if you toed the line. Step out of line, and woe be to you. A cautionary tale that holds true today. Don't slack off on your vigilance people! Get out there and vote!

SPRQ: A History of Ancient Rome, by Mary Beard-

It's surprising how little has really changed other than the weapons. Another surprise to me was how much of the wars in those days were various Roman factions fighting amongst themselves.

The Making of the Atomic Bomb by Richard Rhodes-

A great book on the overview of the development of atomic weapons and their use in WWII. Really good if you like the technical side of things. A long read but worth it.

Catch 22 by Joseph Heller-

A satire on WWII that deals with some of the absurd contradictions that arise in the military—and there are many. One of the characters is named Major Major, and with my last name being Major, I finally read it.

Dispatches by Michael Herr-

One of the first books I read about Vietnam. It captures the feelings of the times through the eyes of a war reporter.

Chickenhawk by Robert Mason -

Great book given from the viewpoint of a Chopper pilot with the 1st Calvary.

War and Peace by Leo Tolstoy -

By the great Russian writer on the invasion of Russia by Napoleon in the 1800s. There is much in this book that is relevant in any age. Get the translation by Pevear/Volohonsky. At over one thousand two hundred pages, you'll have to take a break from social media if you want to ever finish it.

Oxford English Dictionary/Webster's English Dictionary/Latin Dictionary

Save some trees, get one or all of them on your iPhone, or just ask "Alexa".

The Constitution of the United States-

I'm going to include a copy with this book. Get familiar with it!!

Team of Rivals: The Political Genius of Abraham Lincoln-
by Doris Kearns Goodwin.

Check with me later, I'm still chewing through this one. Great book so far.

The Guns of August 1914 by Barbara Tuchman-

Deals with WWI, which was a huge waste of lives on all sides.

The Winds of War-by Herman Wouk

War and Remembrance-also by Herman Wouk

Even though each of these historical fiction books bump up to the nine-hundred-page range, they were good reads. I intend to tackle more of his books at a later date.

We Were Soldiers Once...and Young- by Lt. Gen. Hal Moore/Joe Galloway

Deals with one of the first big set-piece battles in the Vietnamese War. A United States battalion of the 1st Calvary. was almost overrun by four times the numbers of NVA. People started to wake up and give the NVA their due and recognize this was not to be a quick war.

The Bible, Torah, Koran, Bhagavad Gita-
(plus, writings on Buddhism and many more)

Pick one, read, and reread it. Then start on the others. Then go back and learn the languages in which they were originally written for an in-depth understanding and read them again.

The Tunnels of Chu Chi- by Tom Mangold

Deals extensively with the honeycomb of tunnels that are pervasive throughout Vietnam. I've never read it, but I often heard it was a good read.

SR-71- The Complete Illustrated History of The Blackbird, the World's Highest, Fastest Plane by Col. Richard H. Graham, Great book about one of my favorite planes.

Cicero-

Roman lawyer of note who has written extensively (in Latin of course) and is still quoted/referred to this day.

Some Coffee Table Books:

Warriors Remembered, Vietnam Veterans - Welcome Home by Albert J. Napas

Written by a Vietnam veteran of the 101st Airborne Division—a pictorial of Vietnam veteran memorials and the story behind them.

Some National Military Cemeteries:

Great Lakes, Holly, Michigan

Arlington National Cemetery, Arlington, Virginia

Normandy, France (site of the D-Day landings)

Movies:

Das Boot (The Boat)

A German movie about U Boats in WWII. If possible, look at the one in German with English subtext.

Wizard of Oz

From 1939, an American musical fantasy film starring Judy Garland. A hit through the ages. Having said that, I don't think I ever sat through the whole thing from beginning to end.

Saving Private Ryan

Starring Tom Hanks and filmed in 1998. Overall a great movie. It does a good job of portraying combat and is based on actual events.

Bridge on the River Kwai

Based on British POWs of the Japanese who forced to build a bridge as part of the Burma Railway in 1942/43. It won a fair number of Academy Awards.

Flight of the Phoenix, 1965

Make sure you see the one starring James Stewart. The Fairchild C-82 cargo plane featured in the movie is a civilian version of the C-119 boxcar, the first plane I jumped in jump-school while training as a paratrooper. A great cult-movie from my standpoint. I love the part where Jimmy Stewart discovers that the designer who reconfigured their crashed airplane designed model aircrafts and not the full-size versions as he believed. Jimmy had a fit.

The Imitation Game

Starring Benedict Cumberbatch, this is about Allan Turing's life as a Cambridge mathematician recruited by MI6 British Intelligence during WWII to break Nazi codes.

Apocalypse Now, directed by Frances Coppola

I liked the music and some of the scenes, and they captured the sound of the choppers well. Overall, I don't think the director was going so much for accuracy as effect.

Platoon, directed by Oliver Stone

Another blockbuster classic about Vietnam. Right on the money in some scenes. Overall, a pretty good job.

South Pacific

A musical. I saw it with my mom as a kid in Hong Kong. We were passing through there on a return leg of a trip from Indonesia. Part war story/romance/musical. I liked It

Music:

Below are just a few examples of music that have a connection with me.

"Sitting on the Dock of the Bay" by Otis Redding. A big hit ingrained in my mind as it was playing in the background of the EM club as the news was disclosed to me that my friend in my Company has been killed week earlier.

"Platoon Soundtrack"

The Doors

The Beatles

"Black and Blue" by Fats Waller

Samuel Barber

"South Pacific Soundtrack"

"Apocalypse Now Soundtrack"

Maps:

It's worth noting and being aware of the geopolitical situation during the time period during which the Vietnamese war took place. All of China, (excluding Hong Kong and Taiwan), Cambodia, Laos, and many surrounding areas were all off limits. Countries that today could easily be accessed with a relatively inexpensive and quick flight were inaccessible. The unified country that is today Vietnam was then divided in two with a heavily fortified and sealed border, DMZ dividing the North and South.

Some Wars that followed: (Will it ever end?)

Cambodia (the Killing Fields)

Falklands

Rwanda

Bosnia

Iraq/Iran

Kuwait

Afghanistan

Russia/Ukraine

Yemen (Proxy war)

North/South Korea—this one's at a pressure cooker standstill. Somewhat like a simmering semi-active volcano that could blow at any minute!

Thought a truce was signed in 1953, a formal peace was never declared?! Tensions/threats bubble and flare up to this day. If nothing else, I strongly suggest that we avoid getting into new wars before old ones have been brought to a close.

Computers/keyboard:

I owe my start to the typewriter and the class I took in high school, which in time led to computers/word processing software, otherwise I doubt if this book would have seen the light of day. No way could I have had the patience to do all on this writing/editing on a yellow legal pad and a number 2 pencil.

Recent developments leading up to the publishing of this version II of my book *Vietnam Unplugged*...

Cobo Hall in Detroit that I mentioned earlier, has undergone changes and is now called the TFC Convention Center. Gone is the name Cobo, which was the name of a former Detroit Mayor known for his racism.

My brother Brian, also mentioned in the book, passed away and now rests at Great Lakes National Cemetery in Holly, Michigan.

U.S. Space Force: This is a big development! A whole new branch of the military complete with new uniforms and a mandate that literally reaches into space.

Covid-19 turns our Planet upside down and it produced a shift in thinking/priorities.

Above
Sopwith Camel, WW I Fighter Plane,
Fabric over wood frame construction.

Below
Homer Gomez, taken in front of one of our favorite
resupply Choppers. The "nose art" is of little Annie Fanny,
a cartoon character in Playboy magazine at the time.

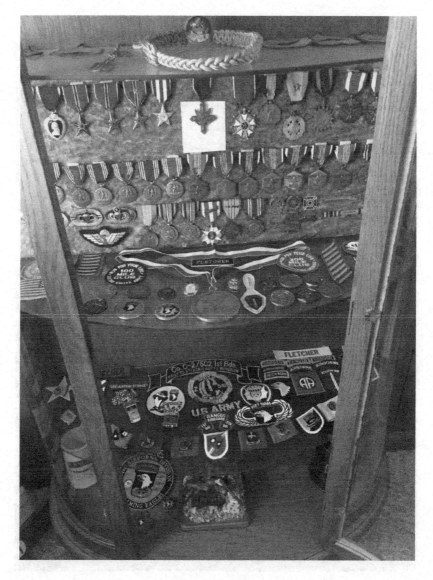

Above
Fletcher's - Same case, different view.

Above
SR-71 Blackbird, shown here at the Smithsonian Museum

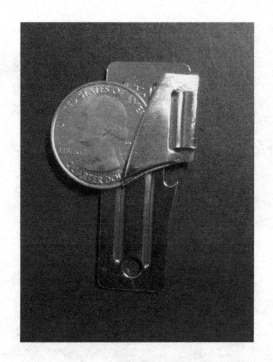

Above
P 38 , can opener

November '67'
101st, 1st Brigade, 2/502, Company C, 3rd Platoon
S.Sgt. Fletcher   G. Garcia   P. Major
            B. Britt   A. Painter   H. Gomez   F. Aragon

Sgt. Perry   Zeke   P. Chagois

Below
The O'Deuce calling cards

ĐÂY LÀ KẾT - QUẢ
CỦA VIỆT CỘNG
NHỮNG NGƯỜI ĐÃ TẠO CHO VỢ HỌ THÀNH
QUẢ PHỤ

COMPLIMENTS OF
THE STRIKE FORCE
WIDOW MAKERS